Pass the Canadian
Citizenship Test!

Canadian Citizenship Test Study Guide and Practice Test Questions

COMPLETE
TEST PREPARATION INC.
WWW.TEST-PREPARATION.CA

We strongly recommend that students check with Citizenship and Immigration Canada for up-to-date information regarding test content.

The only official study guide for the citizenship test is *Discover Canada: The Rights and Responsibilities of Citizenship*, available from Citizenship and Immigration Canada at no cost (http://www.cic.gc.ca/english/resources/publications/discover/). If you have applied for citizenship and are preparing for the citizenship test, your primary resource should be the official study guide.

Citizenship and Immigration Canada are not involved in the production of, and do not endorse this publication.

Published by

Complete Test Preparation Inc.
Victoria BC Canada

Printed in the USA

Version 2.5 March 2019

ISBN-13: 9781928077978

About Complete Test Preparation Inc.

The Complete Test Preparation Team has been publishing high quality study materials since 2005. Over one million students visit our websites every year, and thousands of students, teachers and parents all over the world (over 100 countries) have purchased our teaching materials, curriculum, study guides and practice tests.

Complete Test Preparation is committed to providing students with the best study materials and practice tests available on the market. Members of our team combine years of teaching experience, with experienced writers and editors, all with advanced degrees.

Feedback

We welcome your feedback. Email us at feedback@test-preparation.ca with your comments and suggestions. We carefully review all suggestions and often incorporate reader suggestions into upcoming versions. As a Print on Demand Publisher, we update our products frequently.

https://www.facebook.com/CompleteTestPreparation/

https://www.youtube.com/user/MrTestPreparation

Contents

Getting Started

Below is some basic information about applying for Canadian citizenship.   Please note this is a very general overview of requirements and is NOT a complete or comprehensive list. For a complete list of requirements, please contact Citizenship and Immigration Canada. (http://www.cic.gc.ca/)

Eligibility

To be eligible to become a Canadian citizen, you must satisfy the following conditions:

- age

- permanent resident status

- lived in Canada for 3 years

- language skills

- criminal history (prohibitions)

- Knowledge of Canada and Canadian history

If you have served in the Canadian Armed Forces, you may be able to apply through a fast-track process.

Age

You must be at least 18 years old. For a child under 18:

- you must be the child's parent, adoptive parent or legal guardian,

- the child must be a permanent resident, and

- one parent must be a Canadian citizen or apply to become a citizen at the same time (this also applies to adoptive parents).

Permanent Resident Status

You must have permanent resident (PR) status in Canada. Your PR status must not be in question. That means you must **not** be:

- under review for immigration or fraud reasons

- under a removal order

- You do not need to have a PR card to apply for citizenship. If your PR card has expired, you can still apply for citizenship.

Time you have lived in Canada

You must have resided in Canada for at least three years (1,095 days) in the past four years before you apply. This does not apply to children under 18.

You may be able to count time spent in Canada before becoming a permanent resident, if it was during the past four years.

Language

English and French are Canada's two official languages. You must be able to speak one of the two official languages to apply. You must be able to:

- Use English or French in everyday conversations about common topics

- understand simple instructions, questions and directions

- use basic grammar, including simple structures and tenses

- answer questions and express yourself.

A citizenship officer will interview you, and will assess your language skills during the interview.

Criminal History

You cannot become a citizen if you:

- have been convicted of, or are currently charged with a criminal offence or an offence under the Citizenship Act in the last three years

- are in prison, on parole or probation

- are under a removal order

Knowledge of Canada

To become a citizen, you must understand the rights, responsibilities and privileges of citizenship, such as voting in elections and obeying the law. You must also show you understand Canada's,

- history

- values

- institutions

- symbols

Your Responsibilities

In Canada, the rights of citizenship comes with responsibilities.

As a Canadian Citizen, you must:

- **Obey the law** — One of Canada's founding principles is the rule of law. No person or group are above the law.

- **Take responsibility for yourself and your family** — Finding a job taking care of your family are important Canadian values.

- **Jury duty** — As a Canadian citizen, you are legally required to serve on a jury.

- **Voting** — Voting is a responsibility of all citizens, to help make our democracy function effectively.

Protecting and enjoying Canadian heritage and the environment — Every citizen has a role to play in avoiding waste and pollution while protecting Canada's natural, cultural and architectural heritage for future generations. [1]

Get Answers and Help!

For answers to common questions concerning citizenship, your application and more, visit Citizenship and Immigration Canada online help http://www.cic.gc.ca/english/helpcentre/index-featured-can.asp

Oath of Citizenship

The Oath of Citizenship, or Citizenship Oath, is a statement recited and signed by candidates who wish to become citizens of Canada. Assigned officers preside over a ceremony and administer the oath of fealty to the Canadian monarch and a promise to abide by Canada's laws and customs. After signing the oath, citizenship is granted.

The vow's roots lie in the oath of allegiance taken in the United Kingdom, the modern form of which was implemented in 1689 by King William II and III and Queen Mary II and was inherited by, and used in Canada before 1947. With the enactment of the Citizenship Act that year, the Canadian Oath of Citizenship was established. Proposals for modification of the oath have surfaced from time to time, including removing references to the sovereign, adding loyalty to societal principles, and adding specific mention to Canada. It has, however, only been modified once, in 1977.[2]

Canadian Oath of Citizenship

I swear (or affirm)
That I will be faithful
And bear true allegiance
To Her Majesty Queen Elizabeth the Second
Queen of Canada
Her Heirs and Successors
And that I will faithfully observe
The laws of Canada
And fulfil my duties as a Canadian citizen.

Who we are

Our Ancestors

Thousands of years ago, when Canada was yet unsettled, a small group of people migrated to the great northern land. These pioneers, known as Aboriginals, are believed to have been of Asian descent. Before European and North American explorers even set foot on Canadian soil, these Aboriginals began building a society; one that stood on firm foundations. Inspired by the landscape, these first Canadians structured their lives around religion, nature, and their relationship with the environment. These ideas still hold great importance today.

Many years after these first settlements were established, European explorers made their way into Canada. They were cautious of the Aboriginal people and treated those first Canadians harshly. The Europeans seized land and drove the native settlers north, where the landscape was cruel and unforgiving. Things began to change, however, when King George III initiated the Royal Proclamation of 1863, which guaranteed property rights to native settlers. Despite this decree, the Aboriginal peoples were still treated poorly for many years.

Even as recently as the 19th century, Aboriginals were punished for their heritage. Aboriginal children were placed in schools designed to integrate them into society, but even these children were badly treated, and some were even physically abused. The poor handling of the situation was officially recognized in 2008, when Ottawa officially apologized to the former students.

Today, things are very different. Aboriginals have made significant strides in such areas as education, agriculture, and business. Confident and proud of their heritage, these descendants of the first Canadians now play a critical role in Canadian society.

Three unique groups

The Aboriginals, the first settlers of Canada, are divided into three distinct groups of people: Indians, Inuit, and Métis. Indian refers to all non-Inuit, non-Métis people groups. Often called First Nations, a term coined in the 1970s, the First Nations occupied many of the land reserves throughout Canada and has a large urban population. The term "indian" is no longer used; "First Nations" is the preferred term.

The Inuit, or "the people" in the Inuktitut language, are spread throughout the arctic regions of Canada. Their vast knowledge of nature and the environment has allowed them to thrive in the coldest regions of Canada. Almost three quarters of Inuit in Canada live in Inuit Nunangat. Inuit Nunangat stretches from Labrador to the Northwest Territories and comprises four regions: Nunatsiavut, Nunavik, Nunavut and the Inuvialuit region. The Inuit make up roughly 4% of the native population.

The Inuvialuit are western Canadian Inuit who remained in the Northwest Territories when Nunavut split off. They live primarily in the Mackenzie River delta, on Banks Island, and parts of Victoria Island in the Northwest Territories. They are officially represented by the Inuvialuit Regional Corporation and, in 1984, received a comprehensive land claims settlement, the first in Northern Canada, with the signing of the Inuvialuit Final Agreement.

In September 1992, a final agreement was reached with the Government of Canada. This agreement called for the separation of the Northwest Territories into an eastern territory whose Aboriginal population would be predominately Inuit, the future Nunavut, and a rump Northwest Territories in the west. It was the largest land claims agreement in Canadian history. In November 1992, the Nunavut Final Agreement was approved by nearly 85% of the Inuit of what would become Nunavut. As the final step in this process, the Nunavut Land Claims Agreement was signed on May 25, 1993, in Iqaluit by Prime Minister Brian Mulroney and by Paul Quassa, the president of Nunavut Tunngavik Incorporated. The Canadian Parliament passed the supporting legislation in June of the same year, enabling the 1999 establishment of Nunavut as a territorial entity. [3]

The Métis, a unique population of Aboriginal and European descent, make up about 30% of the native population. Most Métis once spoke, and many still speak Metis French, or a mixed language, Michif. Most the Métis occupy the Prairie provinces of Canada.

Terminology

Aboriginal is an all-encompassing term that includes Inuit, First Nations (Indians), and Métis.

"First Peoples" is also an all-encompassing term that includes Inuit, First Nations (Indians) and Métis.

Aboriginal and First Nations are NOT interchangeable terms.

"Aboriginal" and "First Peoples" ARE interchangeable terms.

Inuit is the contemporary term for "Eskimo."

First Nation is the contemporary term for "Indian."

Inuit are "Aboriginal" or "First Peoples," but are not "First Nations," because "First Nations" are Indians. Inuit are not Indians.

The term "Indigenous Peoples" is an all-encompassing term that includes the Aboriginal or First Peoples of Canada, and other countries. For example, the term "Indigenous Peoples" is inclusive of Inuit in Canada, Maori in New Zealand, Aborigines in Australia. The term "Indigenous Peoples" is generally used in an international context. The title of the United Nations Declaration of the Rights of Indigenous Peoples is a prime example of the global inclusiveness of the term "Indigenous Peoples."

Diversity

Language

Canada consists of two major languages, English and French. Stemming from the early English and French-speaking Christian populations migrating from Europe, the dual-language system is at the center of Canadian education, business, and government. In fact, the Canadian government must, by law, provide services in both English and French.

The 18 million Anglophone, those with English as their first language, make up most of Canada's population. Most of the 7 million Francophone, (about 10-15 percent of the population) those whose first language is French, live in Quebec, though many make their homes in Ontario, New Brunswick, and Manitoba as well. New Brunswick is the only official bilingual province, where English and French serve as co-official languages.

The two major Francophone populations, the Acadians and the Québécois, both find their heritage in early French settlers of Canada. The Acadians are descendants of French seafarers, who settled in the coastal regions of Canada in 1604. The war between France and Britain in the mid-18th century saw much of this population deported, but despite what is known as the "Great Upheaval," a strong Acadian population still calls Canada home.

The Québécois are the people of Quebec, and the vast majority are Francophone. These descendants of 17th and 18th century French settlers are known for their own distinct identity and culture. In 2006, The House of Commons officially recognized the Quebecois as a nation within the united Canada, and they continue to play an integral part in the culture of Quebec.

The Anglophone centers of Canada are generally made up of English, Irish, Welsh, and Scottish, settlers, who migrated to Canada between the 16th and 20th centuries. The foundations of Canada were built on the hard work of such individuals.

Along with speakers of English and French, Canada is also home to a diverse population of speakers of other languages. In Vancouver, for example, an estimated 13% of the population speaks an Asian languages at home.

Canada's history of English and French interaction is one its defining characteristics. The *Official Language Act* of 1969, an act started by Canada's Parliament, has three primary objectives:

- French and English equality in Parliament and other government institutions
- Develop and support language minority communities
- Support French and English equality in Canadian society.

Language Requirements for Canadian Citizenship

To become a Canadian citizen, an individual must have adequate knowledge of English and French, the two official languages of Canada. This requirement is only enforced for individuals under the age of 55.

Ethnicity and Religion

Canada is known for its linguistic heritage, but over the last 200 years it has become a center for ethnic and cultural diversity as well. Often called "the land of immigrants," Canada has become home for millions from a variety of backgrounds. Most immigrants come from European nations (England, France, Scotland, etc.), but, since 1970, the population of Asian immigrants has grown significantly. These men and women continue to shape the Canada of today, and their children provide great hope for the future.

With a variety of ethnic backgrounds comes an assortment of religious beliefs. Christianity is the religion of the majority, with the largest affiliation being Catholic. The next largest group is made up of various Protestant denominations, but the number of Muslims, Jews, Hindus, and those professing no religion continues to grow. Canada has worked with religious institutions throughout its history to promote social welfare and an attitude of tolerance.

Freedom of religion is one of the "Fundamental Freedoms" guaranteed by the Canadian Charter of Rights and Freedoms, which states:

Everyone has the following fundamental freedoms:

> (a) freedom of conscience and religion;
> (b) freedom of thought, belief, opinion and expression, including freedom of the press and other media of communication;
> (c) freedom of peaceful assembly; and
> (d) freedom of association.

Canadians are free to have their own beliefs and opinions, free to practise religion or not as they choose, and free to create organizations with or, without religious ideas. Canadian religious institutions generally benefit from charitable organization status, which allows supporters to receive tax credits, or deductions for their financial contributions.

Besides religious freedom, Canada also maintains a policy of social tolerance. Canadian law supports the gay and lesbian population, specifically in terms of equal treatment and civil marriage. Canada is committed to the support and growth of its diverse population.

Our History

The Aboriginals

The earliest settlers of Canada, the First Peoples, were dependant on the land for their livelihood. Hunters, fisherman, and farmers by trade, the First Nations were masters of their environment. As they sought more resources for growing populations, war became common as tribes came into contact. Groups competed, and tribes grew, but when the Europeans arrived, everything changed.

The arrival of the Europeans brought new products and the possibility of trade, but it also brought disease. Early on, huge populations of the First Nations died. As their interactions continued, however, the onset of diseases decreased and the bonds of trade were formed. European traders, missionaries, and soldiers arrived year after year, laying the foundation for the future of Canada.

The Europeans

The Vikings were the first Europeans to land on what was to become Canadian shores. The remains of their first settlements can still be seen today. These seafarers, who also likely settled Greenland, landed in Labrador and Newfoundland. The Vikings were only the beginning.

European exploration of Canada began in 1497. John Cabot was the first to map Canada's Eastern shore, and less than a century later, another famous explorer, Jacques Cartier, led three more expeditions across the Atlantic to what is today Eastern Canada. Cartier claimed the land for King Francis I of France and on hearing the Iroquois word, *kanata*, ('village'), the land came to be known as Canada.

Royal New France

The first European settlement of what is now Canada, was established by French explorers Pierre de Monts and Samuel de Champlain. These settlements, built in the Bay of Fundy on Île Ste-Croix (Dochet Island) on what's now the Maine-New Brunswick border. This settlement did not survive the harsh winter, and was followed by a settlement at Port-Royal, in Acadia, today, Nova Scotia.

These settlements were followed in 1608 by a fortress in what is now Québec City. With the allegiance of several local Aboriginal tribes, the Algonquin, Montagnais, and Huron, the French colonists were able to survive harsh conditions and establish a healthy trade with the First Nations. This alliance allowed the French to expand, and eventually, gaining control of vast tracts of lands stretching from the Hudson Bay to the Gulf of Mexico.

Early Struggles

While France controlled trade near the Hudson Bay area, England was encroaching into their territory. Tensions were high as the Hudson's Bay Trading Company, given exclusive rights by the King Charles the II of England in 1670, began competing with other trading companies in Montreal. England's hold on the East coast grew quickly and it was soon too powerful for the struggling New France. Tensions build, and in the 18th century, things finally reached a head.

England won a decisive victory in the Battle of the Plains of Abraham at Québec city in 1759, ending the reign of France in Canada and North America. The British renamed the (French) colony at Québec City, now under British administration, "The Province of Quebec," and the French who lived there, Canadiens.

British Accommodation

After their defeat at the hands of the British, the French

population in Québec City was still a majority in the new province. To govern this population, most whom were also Catholic, the British government passed the Quebec Act in 1774. This act served as a middle ground and gave the French Catholics religious freedom and allowed them to run for public office, which was not even possible in Great Britain. The Quebec Act also gave the French the opportunity to exercise civil law, while still being governed by British criminal law.

The American Revolution

In 1776, 13 British colonies to the south of Quebec declared independence from the British. Those who were still loyal to Great Britain, called *Loyalists*, fled to Nova Scotia and Quebec. This group of more than 40,000, consisted of a variety of ethnic, linguistic, and religious backgrounds. 3,000 black Loyalists also moved north, fleeing the ongoing conflict. Some of these black Loyalists, former slaves, founded Freetown, Sierra Leone, a West African colony for freed slaves.

Democracy: The beginning

Establishing democracy, normally a long and bloody process, was for Canada gradual and peaceful. 1758 saw the first representative assembly elected in Halifax, Nova Scotia. Similar elections took place shortly thereafter, including Prince Edward Island (1773) and New Brunswick (1785). Later, the Province of Quebec was split by the *Constitutional Act* (1791) into Lower Canada (present-day Ontario) and Upper Canada (present-day Quebec). In Lower Canada, English-speaking Protestant Loyalists made their homes, and in Upper Canada, French-speaking Catholics. The *Constitutional Act* also formalized the name *Canada*, and gave the people the power to elect legislative assemblies.

The End of Slavery

The process of putting an end to slavery, known as Abolition, began in Canada in the late 18th century. General John Graves Simcoe, a Loyalist military officer, began the push toward Abolition in Upper Canada in 1793. In the following years, the British Parliament would prohibit the buying and selling of slaves and 1883 slavery was abolished in the British Empire. As a result, thousands of slaves from America escaped and headed north into Canada.

Economic Growth

Early on, the fur trade was the most prominent form of business in Canada. The demand for beaver pelts was especially high for Europeans, and the only supply came from North America. The Hudson's Bay Company was largely in command of this lucrative trade, with outposts from Fort Garry (Winnipeg) to Fort Langley (Vancouver). In the 18th and 19th centuries, financial institutions were opened, and in 1832 the Montreal Stock Exchange was established. These new economic developments helped Canada grow, but most people still depended on farming, fishing, and logging to make a living.

The War of 1812

By the 19th century, Canada was becoming an increasingly powerful part of the British Empire. While the British were fighting off Napoleon Bonaparte, the Americans were devising a plan to conquer Canada. Angry at Britain's interference with trade lanes to Europe, the Americans launched an attack on Canada in 1812. Canada was ready, however, and with the help of the First Nations and, in particular, Shawnee chief Tecumseh, the Canadians defeated the Americans. Over the next few years the Canadians and Americans led brief raids into each other's territory, but the Americans eventually came to respect the Canada's resilience.

Rebellion

Canadian democracy was growing, but not fast enough for
some. In 1837-8, rebels attacked areas near Montreal and
Toronto. Many of these rebels demanded the republican values of America, and some even wanted to become a part of
their southern neighbor. These rebels were unable to overcome British soldiers and Canadian volunteers, however,
and many of them were exiled or hanged for their crimes.
The reformer Lord Durham, an Englishman sent to relay
news of the rebellion, suggested that Upper and Lower Canada become one, governed by what he termed a "responsible
government." This meant that British rule must have the
support of most representatives to govern. He also believed
that uniting the people in common language (English) and
religion (Protestant) were the keys to growing the new country of Canada.

Responsible Government

Upper and Lower Canada were united in 1840, forming the
Province of Canada. The reformers Sir Louis-Hippolyte La
Fontaine, Robert Baldwin, and Nova Scotia's Joseph Howe,
were important figures in developing responsible government. Nova Scotia was the first British North American
colony to adopt full responsible government (1847-8). The
same system is alive today, wherein the assembly must hold
full confidence in the government, which would otherwise be
forced to resign.

Confederation

From 1864 to 1867, Canadian representatives were working hard to establish a new country. Known as the Fathers
of Confederation, these men advanced with the full support
of the British government. Two levels of government, federal
and provincial, were formed, and the Province of Canada was
divided into Ontario and Quebec. Along with New Brunswick
and Nova Scotia, these newly independent provinces formed
the Dominion of Canada. Each province had control over its

own legislature, but major democratic issues would be dealt with together.

On July 1,1867 the British Parliament passed the *Constitution Act* - formerly known as the *British North America Act*, which officially named the Dominion of Canada an independent country. Canada Day, formerly Dominion Day, is a national statutory holiday celebrated in all provinces and territories and a day off for most businesses.

Canada's first prime minister was named in 1867. Scotland-born Sir John Alexander Macdonald had come to Canada as a child. A lawyer and a gifted politician, Macdonald was known for his colorful personality and if you have a $10 bill, you will see his portrait.

The West

In 1869, soon after the Dominion of Canada was formed, Métis tribes from the interior captured Fort Garry and threatened the newly formed country of Canada. Because they were not consulted when Canada took over the Northwest region from the Hudson's Bay Company, these 12,000 Aboriginals prepared for battle. Ottawa met the challenge in 1870, sending soldiers to retake Fort Garry and to restore the West. The leader of the uprising, Louis Riel, was defeated and Canada formed a new province, Manitoba. When the rights of the Métis and Indian tribes were again threatened in the late 19th century, Riel again staged a revolt. Louis Riel was executed for high treason in 1885. He is still seen as defender of Métis and Indian rights.

The Métis uprising forced Prime Minister Macdonald to fortify the Western frontier. As a result, the North West Mounted Police (NWMP) was formed in 1873. Their goal was to negotiate and establish peace with the Indians, and in the process, the NWMP established forts that have since grown into major cities and towns. Today, the Royal Canadian Mounted Police (RCMP) are Canada's national police force and one of the most recognizable symbols of Canadian authority.

Along with a national police force, joining the East and West by railroad was another major development of the late 19th century. Ottawa promised to construct a railroad that reached to the West Coast, and this agreement prompted British Columbia to join Canada in 1871. British and American investors financed the new railroad, and European and Chinese labor built it. The Canadian Pacific Railway was finished in 1885. The CPR is a symbol of Canadian unification and the work of the laborers who built it is still remembered today.

Into the West

The end of the 19th century and the beginning of the 20th century were periods of extreme growth in Canada. An estimated 2 million British and American immigrants made their way into Canada over a period of roughly twenty years. Sir Wilfrid Laurier, the first French-Canadian Prime Minister, whose portrait is on the $5 bill, encouraged a westward migration. The railway made it possible for hundreds of thousands to move West, and it did not take long for a thriving agricultural center to develop.

World War I

When Britain declared war on Germany in 1914, Ottawa formed the Canadian Expeditionary Force of over 600,000 men, mostly volunteers. These Canadian forces proved their valor and in April of 1917, they were instrumental in capturing Vimy Ridge in France. This great victory showed the world that Canada was truly united.

The Canadian Corps, formerly the Canadian Expeditionary Force, was also a major contributor in other major victories throughout the final stages of the World War I. When the war ended in 1918, Canada had gained loyalty from its allies and a newfound national pride from its citizens. Canadians remember veterans each year on November 11th, called "Remembrance Day."

Voting Rights for Women

Early on, voting in the Confederation was the right of white male property owners only. This was common in all democracies in the early 20th century. The right to vote, or women's suffrage, was initiated by Dr. Emily Stowe, the first woman to practice the medicine in Canada. Through her determination, Manitoba granted women the right to vote in 1916.

In the years following, women continued to gain further voting rights. By 1918, most women over the age of 21 were allowed to vote in federal elections. In 1921, the first female Member of Parliament, Agnes Macphail, a farmer and a teacher, was elected.

Post-World War I

Following World War I, the British Empire became the British Commonwealth of Nations, an association of free states. Canada continues to play a key role in this association, along with other states of the Empire such as India and Australia.

The 1920's were a time of great success in Canada, with low unemployment and booming business. The Stock Market Crash of 1929, however, had a devastating effect on Canada's economy and led to the Great Depression. In 1933 over a quarter of the population was unemployed and many businesses were forced to close. Furthermore, in the West, a terrible drought coupled with low grain prices destroyed commerce.

These difficulties set the stage for widespread demands for a government instituted program that would serve as a safety net. A set minimum wage, unemployment insurance, and a central bank were all part of this plan. The Bank of Canada was established in 1934, which brought stability to the failing economy.

World War II

When Hitler forced the world into war in 1939, Canada joined its allies in a fight against tyranny and oppression. Over one million Canadians served in the war, and about 44,000 of these died. The Royal Canadian Air Force (RCAF) provided bombers and fighter planes in the Battle of Britain, and the Royal Canadian Navy (RCN) played a key role in the war at sea. By the end of the war, Canada's Navy had grown into the third largest in the world.

In the Pacific, Japan attacked Canadian occupied Vancouver and British Columbia. After four years of war in the Pacific, Japan eventually surrendered in 1945. Following the war, Canadians of Japanese descent were treated harshly and many were forced to relocate. In 1988, the Government of Canada apologized for this wartime treatment.

Canada Today

After the Second World War, Canada enjoyed growth and prosperity. Protectionist trade policies initiated during the Depression were scaled back, opening new possibilities; the most important of these was the General Agreement on Tariffs and Trade (GATT), which is now the World Trade Organization (WTO). Canada's energy industry also grew with the discovery of oil in Alberta (1947). Economic stability also meant that for the first time, most Canadians were able to afford adequate food, clothing, and shelter. Between 1945 and 1970, Canada grew into one of the most prominent countries in the world. Today, its citizens enjoy one of the world's highest standards of living.

Canada's social healthcare program, created with the *Canada Health Act*, is a model for much of the world. Employment insurance, pension plans, and other social programs have helped Canada become a symbol of success.

International Policies

While Canada's rise has been slow and gradual, the international policies Canada developed built relationships that serve well today. The Cold War of the 60s, 70s, and 80s, was an important period for Canada's dealings on an international scale. Canada allied with other democratic nations to form the North Atlantic Treaty Organization (NATO), and later joined the United Nations (UN). Canadian forces have taken part in a variety of peacekeeping operations, including South Korea in the early 1950s.

The Quiet Revolution

While it was having success abroad, Canada was also undergoing internal changes. In the 1960's, Quebec began a campaign to become an independent country. Many in Quebec felt this was necessary to maintain their unique French heritage. In 1963, Canadian Parliament established the Royal Commission on Bilingualism and Biculturalism, which mandated the use of French and English for services throughout Canada. Canada also helped form *La Francophonie*, an international body of French-speaking countries.

Over the last few decades, Quebec has made numerous attempts to gain independence. It is one of a series of ongoing debates in Canada and the developments will certainly play a key role for years to come.

An Ever Changing Society

In a world of ever-changing attitudes and values, Canada continues to show its willingness to adapt. Canada has become known for its flexibility and tolerance, and has attracted people from all over the world. Opportunities for secondary and post-secondary education are widespread in Canada, and many schools have a large international student population.

Over the past century, Canada has also been a haven for refugees from oppressive societies including the former Soviet Union and Vietnam. By 1960, in fact, roughly one third of the Canadian population had roots that were neither British nor French. The Canada of today reflects such diversity, especially in the larger cities.

Arts and Culture

Canada's diverse cultural climate has provided the groundwork for a growing art scene. Many famous novelists, poets, educators, and musicians have drawn inspiration from Canadian diversity. Famous writers like Joy Kogawa and Rohinton Mistry, and musicians including Sir Ernest Macmillan and Healey Willan, have added a rich history of artistry to the already dynamic society.

In the visual arts, Canada is often recognized for the Group of Seven, an assembly of artists who captured the essence of Canada's natural environment. Canada also has an established history of performing arts, with film makers like Denys Arcand and Norman Jewison providing major contributions.

Sports are very popular among Canadians, and Canadian athletes are now recognized as some of the finest in the world. James Naismith invented basketball in 1891, Donovan Bailey won two Olympic gold medals in track and field, and Wayne Gretzky is considered by many to be the greatest hockey player in history.

The most inspirational athlete in Canada, however, was not a professional. In 1980, Terry Fox, an 18-year-old cancer survivor, inspired millions when he began a cross-country run to raise funding and awareness for cancer research. Outside the world of sports, Canada is also an advancing powerhouse in science and technology. Canadian scientists and researchers have won international awards and Canadian schools of science and technology attract the brightest minds from around the world. Alexander Graham Bell, the inventor of telephone technology, may be the most famous of them all. Since 1989, the Canadian Space Agency has also garnered praise for its continuing exploration of our solar system.

Canada's Legal System

Canada's legal and judiciary system is based on the presumption of innocence. This means that every individual is innocent until proven guilty. Individuals are also guaranteed due process, meaning that the government will respect and protect their legal rights.

The Laws of Canada are put into effect by elected representatives. A strong national and local police network enforce the laws and a system of courts and court officials settle legal disputes. Canadian laws govern everyone from the highest officials to the average citizen. These laws are intended to preserve peace and maintain the values of Canada's citizens.

Canada's court system begins at the top with the Supreme Court. The Supreme Court presides of federal matters and important cases related to the government and its branches. Matters that are not federal are handled by smaller provincial and territorial courts. There are a variety of smaller courts, which includes the appeal court, traffic court, and small claims court.

Like the court system, Canada's police force maintains the rights of Canada's citizens. National and local police forces help with all matters related to the violation of Canada's laws. If a citizen of Canada witnesses, or is the victim of a crime, it is their duty to notify the Police. Canada also has a system in which a citizen may dispute any charge filed against them.

If a citizen is summoned to court for a violation of some kind, lawyers are available for assistance. Citizens can hire lawyers on their own, but if the cost is too high, most communities have legal aid services available at little to no cost.

Canada's Economy

Canada's history is one of trade and international commerce. Trade with other nations has made it possible for Canada to grow into one of the most successful countries in the world. Canada's system of free trade with the United States, which began in 1988, has also been a major factor in Canada's economic growth. The North American Free Trade Agreement (NAFTA) of 1994 broadened this former trade agreement and allowed Mexico to become a trading partner. Along with the U.S., Germany, The United Kingdom, Italy, France, Japan, and Russia, Canada is part of the G8 group of the world's top leaders of industry.

Main Industries

Canada's service industry includes education, transportation, construction, health care, tourism, banking, communication, and government. This industry is responsible for employing more than 75% of Canada's workforce.

Canada's manufacturing industries build and distribute products throughout Canada and around the world. Products include, paper, technology-related equipment, automobiles, food, and clothing.

Canada's natural resource industry has played a vital role in Canada's development and it will continue to provide Canada with the means to advance. Forestry, agriculture, fishing, mining, and energy are important industries, and Canada is one of the world leaders in exporting natural resource commodities.

The United States is Canada's leading trade partner, and their partnership has grown into the biggest two-way trade relationship in the world. Over 75% of Canada's exports are bound for the U.S. Billions of dollars' worth of goods cross what is known as "the world's longest undefended border" every year. The Peace Arch in Blaine, Washington, symbolizes the close ties that connect Canada and the U.S.

Canada's Government

Constitutional Monarchy

Canada holds the traditional values of a *constitutional monarchy*, in which the Head of State is the Sovereign (King or Queen). This individual rules according the Canada's Constitution, which is the document outlining the rule of law. The Sovereign's role varies, but generally Her Majesty is a symbol of Canadian heritage and a reflection of Canada's rich history.

A distinction must be made between the Sovereign, who is the head of state, and the Prime Minister, who is the head of government. Canada's Governor General serves as the Sovereign's representative, and his or her term is usually limited to five years. Lieutenant Governors serve as Sovereign representatives in each of the ten provinces.

Levels of Government

Self-Governance

Canada's government has three levels: federal, provincial, territorial/municipal. The interaction of these three branches, the Federal, Judicial, and Legislative branches is critical to Canadian democratic policy, and by working together they are able to secure the rights and freedoms of Canadian citizens.

The federal government is responsible for matters of both national and international scope. This includes defense, foreign policy, and criminal law. Matters such as health, education, and civil rights, are the responsibility of each province. There are also some matters that are shared between the provinces and the federal government, including agriculture and immigration. Canada's system of Federalism allows each province the freedom to govern its own population, which reflects Canada's overall attitude of flexibility.

Canada's government is known as a *Parliamentary Democracy*. This means that the people elect representatives to the provincial and territorial legislatures, as well as to the House of Commons in Ottawa. Members of Parliament, or MPs, carry out such duties as passing laws, monitoring and approving government spending, and keeping the responsibilities of the government front and center. The so-called "confidence of the House" is also an important characteristic of cabinet ministers. If these officials are defeated in a non-confidence vote, they are forced to resign.

Just as the government is divided into three levels, so too is the Parliament. These three parts are the Sovereign (King or Queen), the Senate, and the House of Commons. The Prime Minister, the figurehead of government, selects Cabinet ministers and is tasked with the general operations and procedures of the government. The House of Commons represents the people and is made up of elected members of Parliament. Senators, who may serve until the age of 75, are chosen by the Governor General, who is counseled by the Prime Minister. For any bill to become a law, it must be accepted by both the House of Commons and the Senate, while also receiving royal assent from the Governor General.
The government of Canada, like all democracies, is based on the will of the people. It is therefore important for everyone of voting age to participate, in order that every voice may be heard.

The Federal Government

The federal level (from the Latin foedus, meaning league) of government deals with areas of law listed in the Constitution Act, 1867 and that generally affect the whole country.

At the Federal level, Members of Parliament (MPs) are elected.

Examples of the Federal level of government's responsibilities include, national defence, foreign policy, citizenship, policing, criminal justice, trade and the environment.

Provincial Government

The Provincial level (from the Latin provincia, meaning under Roman rule: from pro, to be in favour of something, and vincere, to conquer) and the territorial level (from the Latin terra, meaning land).

At the Provincial level, Members of the Legislative Assembly (MLAs) are elected.

An individual known as the *Premier* serves the role as the Prime Minister in each province or territory. In the three territories, the *Commissioner*, a representative of the federal government, also plays an important role in the legislature.

Depending on the province or territory, these individuals may be called members of one of the following:

- Legislative Assembly (MLA)

- National Assembly (MNA)

- Provincial Parliament (MPP)

- House of Assembly (MHA)

The 10 provinces and 2 territories share some responsibilities with the Federal government, such as, immigration, agriculture, and the environment.

Examples of Provincial responsibilities include, education, health care, natural resources, highways as well as property and civil rights.

Federal Elections

Federal elections in Canada are held every four years on the third Monday in October. It is, however, possible for the Prime Minister to call an earlier election. There are 308 electoral districts in Canada, each represented by a Member of Parliament (MP), elected by the resident of each electoral district to the House of Commons.

An individual who runs for office is called a candidate. There can be many candidates in each election, but these individuals must be over the age of 18. The candidate who receives the most votes becomes the representative for that electoral district.

Every Vote Counts

The right to vote is a privilege that has been fought over for many years. In Canada, you are given the right to vote if you are the following:

- A Canadian Citizen

- At least 18 years of age

- Registered on the voting list

Elections Canada is an independent, non-partisan agency responsible for conducting federal elections and referendums.

The voting list refers to a database produced by Elections Canada. This is done to ensure that individuals meet the requirements above before they cast their ballot.

When an election has been organized, or called, each registered voter receives information in the mail that tells them where and when the vote will take place, and provides phone numbers for those in need of additional services. Even if an individual does not appear in the database, called the National Register of Electors, there is still an opportunity to be added to the voter list at any time (including on election day).

Another very important Canadian policy is the secret ballot. This rule ensures that every vote is cast in private, and no one may demand that you say who you voted for.

After the voting is cast and the election is over, the leader of the party with the most seats in the House of Commons is appointed by the Governor General. The leader of this party becomes the Prime Minister, and if more than half the seats in the House of Commons supports the party in power, it is called a majority government; if less than half, a minority government.

With the support of the Members of Parliament, the Prime Minister runs the government along with his or her party. This individual must, however, maintain a vote of confidence by the MPs, or the Prime Minister will be defeated and a new election is called.

The Prime Minister is responsible for selecting Cabinet ministers, who run each department of the federal government. Working together with the Prime Minister, these ministers make laws, manage budgets, and make other major decisions.

Those who are not members of the party in power are called opposition parties. These parties are important because they provide different viewpoints on critical issues, which helps the government to solve problems in a way that serves the majority. There are three major parties in Canada: The Conservative Party, the New Democratic Party, and the Liberal Party.

Canada's Symbols

Canada has a rich and storied history. The traditions of Canada extend back hundreds of years and representing this heritage is often done through symbols. Symbols can be objects, pictures, or terms that stand for something greater.

The Crown

The Canadian Crown represents Canada's history as a constitutional monarchy and has been a national symbol for 400 years. Queen Elizabeth II has been the Queen of Canada since 1952, but the crown represents not only the Queen, but the entire Canadian government. This includes Parliament, legislatures, courts, and Canada's Armed Services.

Flags

The red and white pattern of the Canadian flag first represented the Royal Military College, Kingston, in 1867. Red and white are also the traditional colors of France and England, key pieces of Canada's history. The Union Jack of Britain is Canada's official Royal Flag, and many provinces and territories have unique flags of their own which represent a variety of themes.

The Maple Leaf

The Maple Leaf, possibly Canada's most recognizable symbol, was adopted by French Canadians in the 18th century. This symbol has appeared on military uniforms and on the grave stones of fallen soldiers for the past few centuries.

The Fleur-De-Lys

French for "the lily flower," the Fleur-De-Lys has represented French loyalty since 496. The symbol was revived during Confederation, and since then Quebec has adopted the symbol for use on its own flag.

Coat of Arms

After WWI, Canada adopted an official coat of arms, which represents national honor and pride. Along with the coat of arms is the motto, *A mari usque ad mare*, which means "from sea to sea." Symbols of England, France, and Scotland are all part of the coat of arms, which can be seen today on Canadian currency, legal documents, and government buildings.

Parliament Buildings

Canada's Parliament buildings are located in Ottawa, Ontario, and their style represents English, French, and Aboriginal traditions. The Center Block of the Complex, which was completed in 1860, was destroyed by fire in 1916. The library is all that remains of the original complex, but the remaining buildings were reconstructed in 1922. The Peace Tower, the most prominent building, contains the Books of Remembrance, a list of all Canadian military personnel who died during service. The provincial legislatures are also notable for their architectural style, with Quebec's National Assembly being the prime example.

Traditions of Sport

Hockey is Canada's most popular sport and is the official sport of winter. Developed in the 19th century, ice hockey is a popular sport among children, and in summer it is often played on streets and in parks. The National Hockey League (NHL), is the most popular spectator sport in Canada, and many of the best professional players are Canadian. Professional men compete for the Stanley Cup, the trophy awarded to the league champion, while women compete for the Clarkson Cup. The Stanley Cup is named after Governor General Lord Stanley, and the Clarkson after Governor General Adrienne Clarkson.

Other popular sports in Canada include Curling, in which players direct stones down a lane of ice to score points, and Lacrosse, the official summer sport. Lacrosse is the traditional game of Canada's Aboriginals, and is similar to hockey in many ways. Despite the popularity of these sports, soccer has the highest number of registered players in Canada.

The Beaver

The beaver, a former symbol of the Hudson's Bay Company, became the official emblem of St. Jean Baptiste Society in 1834. In the 19th and 20th centuries the symbol of the beaver became a popular choice for other organizations as well. Today, the beaver can be seen on the five-cent coin, the coat of arms for Alberta and Saskatchewan, and cities including Montreal and Toronto.

The Victoria Cross

The Victoria Cross is the highest military honor available in Canada. It is awarded to individuals who displayed extreme bravery, devotion, and valor, in the presence of an enemy. Since 1854, 96 Canadians have received this award.

The National Anthem

O Canada was proclaimed as the national anthem in 1980. It was first sung in Québec City in 1880. French and English Canadians sing different words to the national anthem.

O Canada
O Canada! Our home and native land!
True patriot love in all thy sons command
With glowing hearts we see thee rise
The true North strong and free!
From far and wide, O Canada
We stand on guard for thee
God keep our land glorious and free!
O Canada, we stand on guard for thee
O Canada, we stand on guard for thee

Ô Canada
Ô Canada! Terre de nos aïeux,
Ton front est ceint de fleurons glorieux!
Car ton bras sait porter l'épée,
Il sait porter la croix!
Ton histoire est une épopée
Des plus brillants exploits.
Et ta valeur, de foi trempée,
Protégera nos foyers et nos droits.

Protégera nos foyers et nos droits.

Royal Anthem

The Royal Anthem of Canada, "God Save the Queen (or King)," can be played or sung on any occasion
when Canadians wish to honour the Sovereign.

God Save the Queen
God save our gracious Queen!
Long live our noble Queen!
God save the Queen!
Send her victorious,
Happy and glorious,
Long to reign over us,
God save the Queen!

Dieu protège la Reine
Dieu protège la Reine!
De sa main souveraine!
Vive la Reine!
Qu'un règne glorieux,
Long et victorieux,
Rende son peuple

Statutory Holidays

Date	English name	French Name	Remarks
January 1	New Year's Day	*Jour de l'An*	Celebrates the first day of every year in the Gregorian calendar.
Friday before Easter Day	Good Friday	*Vendredi saint*	Commemorates the crucifixion of Jesus. In Quebec, non-federally regulated employers must give either Good Friday or Easter Monday as a statutory holiday, though some give both days.

July 1 (July 2 when July 1 is a Sunday)	Canada Day	*Fête du Canada*	Celebrates Canada's 1867 Confederation and establishment of dominion status. In Newfoundland and Labrador, observed as Memorial Day.
First Monday in September	Labour Day	*Fête du travail*	Celebrates economic and social achievements of workers.
December 25	Christmas Day	*Noël*	Celebrates the Nativity of Jesus.

4

Canada's Regions

At roughly 10 million square kilometers, Canada is the second largest country on earth. Canada is bordered by the Pacific Ocean in the West, the Atlantic Ocean in the East, and the Arctic Ocean in the North. It also shares its southern border with the U.S., and both countries remain committed to peaceful relations and a secure border.

Canada is made up of five unique and distinct regions: The Atlantic Provinces, Central Canada, The Prairie Provinces, The West Coast, and The Northern Territories. Canada is further divided into three territories and ten provinces. It is important to know the capitals of each province and territory. The Capital of Canada is Ottawa, a major metropolitan and political center bordered by the Ottawa River to the north. Ottawa was chosen as the capital by Queen Victoria in the year 1857. Canada has a population of roughly 34 million people (A 2014 estimate is 35,344,962)

The Atlantic Provinces - Newfoundland and Labrador, Prince Edward Island, Nova Scotia, and New Brunswick.

The Atlantic Provinces

Canada's Atlantic Provinces include Newfoundland and Labrador, Prince Edward Island, Nova Scotia, and New Brunswick.

Newfoundland and Labrador is not only Canada's east-ernmost point, but it is the most easterly point of North America. Because the Atlantic Ocean borders the province, they have a heritage linked to the sea. The unique culture of Newfoundland and Labrador has always been based on fish-ing, but it has more recently been associated with off-shore oil and hydroelectric power.

Prince Edward Island is Canada's smallest Province, and known for its thriving agriculture and beautiful beaches. Prince Edward Island is also known as the birthplace of Confederation, and its world-renowned Confederation Bridge connects the island to the mainland. The famous Lucy Maude Montgomery novel *Anne of Green Gables* is set on Prince Edward Island.

Among the Atlantic Provinces, Nova Scotia has the largest population. The Bay of Fundy in Nova Scotia is known for having the highest tides in the world. Like the other coastal provinces, Nova Scotia has a strong connection with the sea. Shipbuilding, fishing, agriculture, and coal mining, are all major contributors to Nova Scotia's economy and its capi-tal, Halifax, has played an important role in Canada's naval defenses.

New Brunswick is situated in the Appalachian Mountain Range, and has one of the largest river systems in North America. Founded by United Empire Loyalists, New Bruns-wick is known for its rich forestry, agriculture, and tourism industries. New Brunswick is Canada's only official bilin-gual province, with roughly a third of the population speak-ing French for business and every living. Fredericton is the historic capital, and Moncton is the Francophone Acadian center.

Central Canada - Ontario and Quebec

Central Canada

Central Canada includes the provinces of Ontario and Quebec. Central Canada is the manufacturing and industrial center of Canada and more than half the population live the areas around the Great Lakes.

Quebec is populated by nearly eight million people, most whom live near the St. Lawrence River. Over 75% of people in Quebec speak French. The major industries of Quebec include forestry, energy, and mining. Quebec is Canada's leading producer of Hydro-electric power, thanks to its large supply of fresh water. Quebec is also known for its technology industries, especially aeronautics and pharmaceuticals. Montreal, the second largest city in Canada, reflects the cultural diversity that the entire Province is famous for.

Ontario's population of more than 12 million people makes up over one third of Canada's entire population. The economy, culture, and available resources of Ontario play a key role in Canada's infrastructure. Most of Canada's exports come from Ontario, especially manufactured and service industries. Especially known for its success in the agricultural industry, Ontario is home to the famous Niagara wine region. Ontario, like New Brunswick, was founded by United Empire Loyalists, and the province has the second highest population of French speakers. The Great Lakes (Ontario, Erie, Huron, Michigan, Superior) are also located in Southern Ontario.

The Prairie Provinces - Albert, Saskatchewan and Manitoba

The Prairie Provinces

The Prairie Provinces include Alberta, Manitoba and Saskatchewan, and are known for their abundance of natural resources and rich, fertile farmland.

Agriculture, mining, and hydro-electric power production are Manitoba's most important economic offerings. The most famous street intersection, Portage and Main, lies in the city of Winnipeg, Manitoba's most populous city. The area around this intersection is known as the Exchange District. St. Boniface, an area in Winnipeg's French Quarter, has Canada's largest Francophone community at 45,000 people. Manitoba is also known for its large Ukrainian and Aboriginal populations.

Saskatchewan is Canada's largest producer of oil seeds and grains, and was once known as "the breadbasket of the world." Roughly 40% of Canada's arable farmland is located in Saskatchewan, and due to its abundant supplies of uranium and potash. These resources are often found in fertilizers, and help make Saskatchewan a leader in agriculture. The central training facility for the Royal Canadian Mounted

Police is also found in Saskatchewan's capital, Regina. Saskatoon is the largest city in Saskatchewan, the headquarters of the mining industry.

Alberta has the highest population among Prairie Provinces. The Province itself and the world famous Lake Louise are named after the fourth daughter of Queen Victoria, Princess Louise Caroline Alberta. Alberta has five national parks, including the famous Banff National Park, which was established in 1885. Its mountainous terrain has become popular for historians and archaeologists, who continue to discover unique fossils from prehistoric times. Alberta produces more oil and gas than any of Canada's other provinces, and the oil sands in northern Alberta an important resource for Alberta and for Canada. Alberta is also famous for its agriculture and, specifically, beef production.

The West Coast - British Columbia

The West Coast

British Columbia is Canada's western-most province, and has a population of about four million. Victoria is the capital and its location on the Pacific coast has been a major factor in Canada's success in international trade. Billions of dollars of goods are imported and exported every year through ports on the West Coast of BC.

Roughly 50% of all goods produced in British Columbia come from the forestry industry. These products include lumber and paper products, which have made this the most valuable forestry center in Canada. British Columbia is also known for successful mining and fishing industries, as well as the production of fruit orchards and vineyards. British Columbia's most prominent feature is its extensive network of parks. British Columbia contains over 600 provincial parks, which are a popular source of tourism every year.

British Columbia also contains a strong Asian population. Chinese and Punjabi are the most spoken languages after English.

The Northern Territories - The Yukon and
Northwest Territories

The Northern Territories

Despite making up roughly one third of Canada's land mass, the Northern Territories have a population of only 100,000. Mining is the primary industry in the north, as the climate and terrain make other resources difficult to develop and produce. Often called the "Land of the Midnight Sun" due to the long summer and short winter days, The Northern Territories are mostly Arctic Tundra. Hunting, Fishing, and Trapping are also a part of the northern culture, and Inuit Art is an especially popular commodity that is sold through-out the world.

The Yukon is famous for attracting thousands of miners during the gold rush of the 19th century. The White Pass and Yukon railway, built in 1900 to connect several bustling mining centers, has now become a popular tourist excursion. Many passengers depart in neighboring Skagway, Alaska, enjoying scenic views and mountain vistas. Yukon is also notorious for its cold weather and the coldest temperature ever recorded in Canada (-63°C) was taken in the Yukon.

The Northwest Territories were once composed of Rupert's Land and the Northwestern Territory (1870). Yellowknife, its capital is known as the "diamond capital of North America." More than 50% of the population is Aboriginal, and the second longest river in North America, The Mackenzie, flows through the Northwest Territory.

Meaning "our land" in Inuktitut, Nunavut was not established until 1999. The capital of Nunavut is Iqaluit, which as formerly known as Frobisher Bay. Martin Frobisher was an English explorer who was sent into Canada in 1576 by Queen Elizabeth I. Inuktitut is an official language and is, in fact, the first language used in schools. The population of Nunavut is about 85% Inuit.

Capital City	Province or Territory
St. John's	Newfoundland and Labrador
Halifax	Nova Scotia
Fredericton	New Brunswick
Charlottetown	Prince Edward Island
Québec	Quebec
Toronto	Ontario
Winnipeg	Manitoba
Regina	Saskatchewan
Edmonton	Alberta
Victoria	British Columbia
Iqaluit	Nunavut
Yellowknife	Northwest Territories
Whitehorse	Yukon

1. Who are the Aboriginals?

    a. People of Asian descent

    b. European explorers

    c. North American explorers

    d. A small group from the great northern land.

2. Who initiated the Royal Proclamation of 1863?

    a. Queen Victoria

    b. King George III

    c. King George IV

    d. The Government of United Kingdom

3. What are three unique groups of first settlers?

    a. Aboriginals, French and English

    b. Aboriginals, Inuits and Metis

    c. Indians, Inuit, and Métis.

    d. Inuits,French and Métis.

4. What term was used to refer to non-Inuit, non-Métis peoples?

    a. The English

    b. The French

    c. Aboriginals

    d. First Nations

5. Which group makes up about 5% of the Native population?

    a. Inuits and Métis.

    b. Indian

    c. Métis

    d. Inuit

6. Where do most Inuit live?

    a. Throughout Canada

    b. The Arctic regions of Canada

    c. Urban regions of Canada

    d. The Prairie Provinces of Canada.

7. Which group is made up of both Aboriginals and people of European descent?

    a. Inuit

    b. Indians

    c. Metis

    d. Inuits & Metis

8. What language do the Metis speak?

    a. Inuktitut

    b. English

    c. Michif

    d. French

9. Where do the majority of Metis live?

    a. The Prairie Provinces

    b. The Arctic regions

    c. Urban regions of Canada.

    d. Throughout Canada

10. Which dialect is derived from English and French?

    a. Michif

    b. Inuktitut

    c. Cree

    d. Ojibwa

11. Which group makes up almost 30% of the Native population?

    a. Inuits

    b. Indians

    c. Metis

    d. Inuits & Metis

12. What are the two official languages of Canada?

    a. Inuktitut and Michif,

    b. English and Michif

    c. English and French

    d. French and Inuktitut

13. Who are the Anglophones?

    a. People whose first language is English

    b. People whose first language is French

    c. People whose first language is French and English

    d. People whose first language is neither French nor English

14. Who are Francophones?

    a. People whose first language is French

    b. People whose first language is English

    c. People whose first language is French and English

    d. People whose first language is neither French nor English

15. Where do most Francophones live?

    a. Quebec

    b. Ontario

    c. New Brunswick,

    d. Manitoba

16. Acadians and the Québécois are

    a. People of European descent

    b. Two major anglophone populations

    c. Two major francophone populations

    d. The aboriginal who first settled in Canada

17. Who are the descendants of 17th and 18th century French settlers?

    a. The Québécois

    b. The Acadians

    c. The Ontarians

    d. A and B

18. Which nation within Canada was officially recognized by The House of Commons?

    a. The Quebecois

    b. The nation of the Acadians

    c. The United Canada , 2006

    d. Canada

19. What are the descendants of 17th and 18th century French settlers known as?

    a. People of European descent

    b. The Québécois

    c. the Acadians

    d. the Ontarians

20. Where are Asian languages spoken the most?

    a. Quebec

    b. Vancouver

    c. Ontario

    d. Northern Canada

21. What is Canada often called?

a. Land of the immigrants

b. The Great North

c. Land of ethnic diversity

d. Land of cultural diversity

22. Which European nations do most Canadian immigrants come from?

a. England

b. France

c. Scotland

d. All of the above

23. Since 1970, where have a significant number of immigrants come to Canada from?

a. European

b. Asian

c. Great Britain

d. African

24. What is the main religion in Canada?

a. Islam

b. Hinduism

c. Sikhism

d. Christianity

25. What is the second largest religious group in Canada?

a. Hindus

b. Protestants

c. Muslims

d. Jews

26. What religious freedoms do Canadians enjoy?

a. Freedom of religion

b. Freedom of religious expression (customs, ceremonies, etc.),

c. Freedom of conscience

d. All of the above

27. Early in Canadian history, what happened when different tribes came into contact with each other?

a. Increase in conflict

b. Growing resources

c. Declining resources

d. Growing communities

28. Does Canadian law support marriage of homosexuals?

a. Yes

b. No

c. Only in some Provinces

29. Who were the first Europeans to land on Canadian shores?

a. The Aboriginals

b. The Vikings

c. The seafarers

d. European Explorers

30. Where did the Vikings land?

a. Labrador and Newfoundland

b. Greenland and Newfoundland

c. Labrador and Greenland

d. None of the above

31. Who was the first to map Canada's Eastern shore?

a. John Cabot

b. Jacques Cartier

c. Both A & B

d. None of the above

32. What is the origin of the name "Canada?"

a. From the name of the person who founded the country

b. From the Iroquoi word "kanata"

c. From the name of the Explorer

d. From the name of the persons who first set foot in Canada

33. What does the Iroquoi word "Kanata" mean?

a. A Country

b. A Town

c. A village

d. A city

34. What are the first European settlements now called?

a. Quebec City

b. Maine and Quebec City

c. Nova Scotia and Quebec City

d. Maine and Nova Scotia

35. What year was the fortress at Quebec City established?

a. 1806

b. 1680

c. 1608, Champlain

d. 1860

36. Who, or what are The Algonquin, Montagnais, and Huron?

a. Local Aboriginal tribes

b. French Colonies

c. Types of lands

d. Names of villages

37. What does the Remembrance Day poppy symbolize?

a. The founding of Canada

b. The birthday of Canada's prime minister

c. A national holiday

d. The sacrifice made by veterans

38. Who did King Charles II give exclusive trading rights to?

a. Hudson's Bay Trading Company, 1670

b. Trading companies in Montreal

c. Trading companies on the East coast

d. Trading companies owned by the English

39. What year was the Battle of the Plains of Abraham?

a. 1759, Quebec City

b. 1750

c. 1859

d. 1810

40. What was the goal of the formation of the NWMP?

a. To bring law and order

b. To help to establish power in Canada

c. To establish their presence

d. To negotiate and establish peace with the Indians

41. Who renamed Quebec City?

a. The British

b. The French

c. Both A & B

d. None of the above

42. The labor force of which two countries is still remembered for their contribution to building the railroad?

a. European and Chinese labor force, finished 1885

b. European and American labor force

c. European and Canadian labor force

d. Chinese and American labor force

43. Who were the Canadienes?

a. The French who resided in Quebec City

b. The English who resided in Quebec City

c. The tribes of Quebec City

d. None of the above

44. Who passed the Quebec Act ? 1774

a. The Canadian Government

b. The British government

c. The French government

d. French Catholics

45. What is CPR remembered for?

a. Unification of Canada

b. The toil of the labor work force in building the railway project

c. Both A and B

d. Neither A nor B

46. How many British colonies south of Quebec declared independence?

    a. 3

    b. 31

    c. 31

    d. 13

47. What year did the British Colonies in Quebec gain independence?

    a. 1761

    b. 1776

    c. 1767

    d. 1677

48. Which group moved north, away from the ongoing conflict in Quebec?

    a. Different tribes

    b. Black Loyalists — 3600

    c. New group of loyalists

    d. Tribes who migrated from other countries

49. What was the name of the West African colony for freed slaves?

    a. Freetown

    b. Freedom Town

    c. Freecity

    d. Freed Town

50. What year was the first representative assembly elected ?

    a. 1578

    b. 1758 Halifax - N.S.

    c. 1785

    d. 1587

51. When is "Remembrance Day" celebrated in Canada?

    a. November 1

    b. November 10

    c. November 11

    d. November 30

52. In which year were the first elections held in Prince Edward Island?

    a. 1373

    b. 1377

    c. 1737

    d. 1773

53. What year were elections held in New Brunswick?

    a. 1875

    b. 1785

    c. 1758

    d. 1857

54. What caused the split of the Province of Quebec?

    a. The Assembly elections

    b. The Constitutional Act   1791

    c. The institution of Democracy

    d. Geographical reasons

55. What are the present day names for Upper and Lower Canada?

    a. Montreal and Halifax

    b. Quebec and Halifax

    c. Ontario and Quebec

    d. Ontario and Montreal

56. Which group of people made Upper Canada their home?

    a. English-speaking Protestant Loyalists

    b. The Black Loyalists

    c. The English speaking Catholics

    d. French-speaking Catholics

57. Who played a key role in safeguarding the Canadian seas during World War II?

    a. Royal Canadian Navy

    b. Recognized Canadian Navy

    c. Royal Canada Navy

    d. Regional Canadian Navy

58. How was Canada officially given its name?

    a. The elected representatives

    b. The Constitutional Act, 1791

    c. The people of Canada

    d. The various religious groups

59. What was the process of putting an end to slavery called?

    a. Anti-Slavery

    b. Freedom

    c. Abolition

    d. Freedom from Slavery

60. Who was the Loyalist military officer who started the process to end slavery in Upper Canada? 1793

    a. General John Gravas Simcoe

    b. General John Graves Simcore

    c. General John Graves Simcote

    d. General John Graves Simcoe

61. What does Inuit mean?

    a. Another word for Metis.

    b. A territory in northern Canada

    c. Aboriginal people in northern Canada

    d. Aboriginal people in Atlantic Canada

62. What year was slavery abolished?

    a. 1838

    b. 1881

    c. 1388

    d. 1883

63. What are three rights Canadians have?

a. Freedom of religion, peaceful assembly, and association

b. Freedom of religion, marriage, vote

c. Freedom of belief, peaceful assembly and vote

d. Freedom of association, religion and marriage

64. What was the most prominent form of business in Canada's early days?

a. Fur Trading

b. Beaver pelts

c. Farming

d. Dairy Farming

65. What was Vancouver's original name?

a. Hudson's Bay

b. Winnipeg

c. Fort Langley

d. Fort Garry

66. What Canadian commodity was in high demand in Europe?

a. Farming

b. Financial institutions

c. Fur trade

d. Beaver pelts

67. What year was the Montreal Stock Exchange established?

a. 1238

b. 1382

c. 1823

d. 1832

68. Who launched an attack on Canada in 1812?

    a. Napoleon Bonaparte

    b. The British

    c. The Americans

    d. The First Nations

69. Who helped Canada defeat America?

    a. Shawnee chief Tecumseh

    b. The First Nations

    c. Both A & B

    d. None of the above

70. Who attacked areas near Montreal and Toronto in 1837-38?

    a. Canadian rebels

    b. American rebels

    c. British rebels

    d. First Nations rebels

71. What was the outcome of the rebellion in 1837?

    a. Their demands were accepted

    b. Rebels were hung or exiled

    c. The rebellion was successful

    d. The rebellion died

72. What year did Upper and Lower Canada unite?

    a. 1814

    b. 1804

    c. 1840

    d. 1814

73. What was the name given to the union of Upper and Lower Canada in 1840?

    a. Vancouver

    b. Nova Scotia

    c. The First Nations

    d. The Province of Canada

74. Which colony was the first to adopt full responsible government?

    a. Lower Canada

    b. Upper Canada

    c. Nova Scotia

    d. Hudson Bay

75. What were the representatives who established the new country of Canada?

    a. The Fathers of Confederation

    b. British government

    c. Canadian government

    d. Canadian representatives

Answer Key

1. A
Aboriginals are a small group of people who migrated to
what is now Canada. They are believed to be of Asian descent.

2. B
King George III initiated the Royal Proclamation of 1863,
which guaranteed property rights to native settlers.

3. C
The first settlers of Canada, the Aboriginals, included three
groups: Indians, Inuit, and Métis.

4. D
First Nations is the modern term for "indian."

Aboriginal is an all-encompassing term that includes Inuit,
First Nations (Indians), and Métis.

5. D
The Inuit make up roughly 5% of the native population.

6. B
The Inuit, or "the people" in the Inuktitut language, are
spread throughout the arctic regions of Canada. Almost
three-quarters of Inuit in Canada lived in Inuit Nunangat.
Inuit Nunangat stretches from Labrador to the Northwest
Territories and comprises four regions: Nunatsiavut, Nunavik, Nunavut and the Inuvialuit region.

7. C
The Métis is a unique population of Aboriginal and European
descent.

8. C
The Inuit speak a distinctive dialect, Michif.

9. A
Most Métis live in the Prairie Provinces.

10. A
The Metis dialect, Michif, is derived from their English and French-speaking heritage.

11. C
The Métis, a unique population of Aboriginal and European descent, make up about 30% of the native population.

12. C
Canada has two official languages, English and French.

13. A
Anglophones, or English speaking people, make up most Canada's population.

14. A
Francophones, or French speaking people, make up about 10-15 percent of Canada's population.

15. A
Most of the 7 million Francophone, those whose first language is French, live in Quebec.

16. C
Acadians and the Québécois are the two major Francophone populations.

17. D
The Acadians (and the Québécois), are descendents of the early French settlers of Canada.

18. A
In 2006, The House of Commons officially recognized the Quebecois as a nation within the United Canada.

19. B
The Québécois are the descendents of 17th and 18th century French settlers, known for their own distinctive identity and culture.

20. B
Asian languages are spoken the most in Vancouver, where an estimated 13% of the population speak an Asian language at home.

21. A
Canada has become a center for ethnic and cultural diversity, and is often called "the land of immigrants."

22. D
Most immigrants come from European nations (England, France, Scotland, etc.).

23. B
Since 1970, the number of Asian immigrants has grown significantly.

24. D
Christianity is the religion of the majority, with the largest affiliation being Catholic.

25. B
The second largest group is made up of various Protestant denominations.

26. D
The freedoms of religion, religious expression (customs, ceremonies, etc.), and freedom of conscience are all protected by the Canadian Charter of Rights and Freedoms

27. A
As they sought more and more resources for growing populations, war also became common as tribes came into contact.

28. A
Canada has a policy of social tolerance and Canadian law supports the marriage of homosexuals (gays).

29. B
Vikings were the first Europeans to land on Canadian shores.

30. A
Vikings first landed in Labrador and Newfoundland.

31. A
John Cabot was the first to map Canada's Eastern shore.

32. B

Iroquoi word kanata is believed to be the origin of the word Canada.

33. C

The word 'Canada' comes from the Iroquois word 'kanata,' means village.

34. B

The first European settlements were established on what is now the Maine New Brunswick border.

35. C

In 1608 Champlain established a fortress in what is now Québec City.

36. A

The Algonquin, Montagnais, and Huron are local Aboriginal tribes.

37. D

The red poppy symbolizes the sacrifices made by Canadian soldiers who fought in wars to protect Canada.

38. A

King Charles the II of England gave the Hudson's Bay Trading Company exclusive trading rights in 1670.

39. A

The Battle of the Plains of Abraham at Québec city was fought in 1759.

40. D

The goal of the North West Mounted Police (NWMP) was to negotiate and establish peace with the Indians, and in the process the NWMP established forts that have since grown into major cities.

41. A

The British renamed the colony at Québec City "The Province of Quebec" after defeating the French at the Battle of the Plains of Abraham.

42. A
The Canadian Pacific Railway was constructed by a European and Chinese labor force, and finished in 1885.

43. A
After the Battle of the Plains of Abraham, the British named the French who lived in Quebec City Canadiens.

44. B
The British passed the Quebec Act in 1774 to accommodate the majority French population in Quebec.

45. C
The Canadian Pacific Railroad is remembered for uniting the country, and for the work of the laborers who built it.

46. D
13 British colonies to the south of Quebec declared independence.

47. B
In 1776, the 13 British colonies to the south of Quebec declared independence from the British.

48. B
3,000 black Loyalists moved north away from the ongoing conflict.

49. A
Black Loyalists, former slaves, went founded Freetown, Sierra Leone, a West African colony for freed slaves.

50. B
1758 saw the first representative assembly elected in Halifax, Nova Scotia.

51. C
Canadians remember veterans each year on November 11th, which is called "Remembrance Day."

52. D
Elections took place in Prince Edward Island in 1773.

53. B
Elections took place in New Brunswick in 1785.

54. B
The Province of Quebec was split by the Constitutional Act (1791).

55. C
Upper Canada is present-day Ontario and Lower Canada is present-day Quebec.

56. D
French-speaking Catholics made their home in Upper Canada.

57. A
The Royal Canadian Navy (RCN) played a key role in the control of the seas.

58. B
The Constitutional Act of 1791 formalized the name Canada.

59. C
The process of putting an end to slavery was known as Abolition.

60. D
General John Graves Simcoe, a Loyalist military officer, began the push toward Abolition in Upper Canada in 1793.

61. C
Inuit, or "the people" in the Inuktitut language, are spread throughout the arctic regions of Canada.

62. D
The British Parliament would prohibit the buying and selling of slaves and in 1883 slavery was abolished in the British Empire.

63. A
Canadians enjoy the following freedoms:

(a) freedom of conscience and religion;

(b) freedom of thought, belief, opinion and expression, including freedom of the press and other media of communication;
(c) freedom of peaceful assembly; and
(d) freedom of association.

64. A
The fur trade was the most prominent form of business in Canada.

65. C
Fort Langley is the original name of Vancouver.

66. D
Beaver pelts was in high demand in Europe.

67. D
The Montreal Stock Exchange was established in 1832.

68. C
The Americans launched an attack on Canada in 1812.

69. C
Canada, and with the help of the First Nations and, in particular, Shawnee chief Tecumseh, the Canadians were able to defeat the Americans.

70. A
In 1837-8, rebels attacked areas near Montreal and Toronto.

71. B
These rebels were unable to overcome British soldiers and Canadian volunteers, and many were exiled or hanged.

72. C
Upper and Lower Canada were united in 1840.

73. D
Upper and Lower Canada were united in 1840, forming the Province of Canada.

74. C
Nova Scotia was the first British North American colony to

adopt full responsible government.

75. A

The representatives who established the new country of Canada are called the Fathers of Confederation.

Practice Test Questions Set 2

The practice test portion presents questions that are representative of the type of question you should expect to find
on the Canadian Citizenship Exam. **However, they are not
intended to match exactly what is on the exam.**

For the best results, take this Practice Test as if it were the
real exam. Set aside time when you will not be disturbed,
and a location that is quiet and free of distractions. Read
the instructions carefully, read each question carefully, and
answer to the best of your ability.

Use the bubble answer sheets provided. When you have
completed the Practice Test, check your answer against the
Answer Key and read the explanation provided.

Do not attempt more than one set of practice test questions
in one day. After completing the first practice test, wait two
or three days before attempting the second set of questions.

1. Name the two levels of government formed in 1864 - 67?

    a. Federal and Provincial

    b. Federal and Confederation

    c. Confederation and Provincial

    d. Province of Canada and Dominion of Canada

2. Name the two divisions of the Province of Canada

    a. Hudson Bay and Nova Scotia

    b. Ontario and Nova Scotia

    c. Ontario and Quebec

    d. Hudson Bay and Quebec

3. In which year did the British Parliament pass the British North America Act?

    a. 1876

    b. 1867

    c. 1786

    d. 1768

4. What is the former Dominion Day celebration now called?

    a. Independence Day

    b. Freedom Day

    c. Annual Day

    d. Canada Day

5. Who was the **first Prime Minister of Canada?**

    a. Sir John Alexander Macdonald *, 1867 — born in Scotland*

    b. Sir Louis-Hippolyte La Fontaine

    c. Robert Baldwin

    d. Joseph Howe

6. Where is a portrait of the first Prime Minister of Canada?

    a. On a $1 bill

    b. On a $11 bill

    c. On a $10 bill

    d. On a $100 bill

7. How was the Province of Manitoba formed?

    a. By defeating the rebels in the battle at Fort Garry

    b. By getting the Aboriginals to quit the region

    c. From the North West region

    d. From the Hudson Bay Company

8. Who was the leader of the Aboriginals who fought Canada?

    a. Joseph Howe

    b. Lord Durham

    c. Louis Riel

    d. Robert Baldwin

9. What year were the North West Mounted Police (NWMP) formed?

a. 1783

b. 1837

c. 1873

d. 1738

10. Who won the Battle of the Plains of Abraham at Québec city?

a. England (1759

b. France

c. North America

d. Canada

11. What does RCMP stand for?

a. Recognized Canadian Mounted Police

b. Regional Canadian Mounted Police

c. Royal Canadian Mounted Police

d. Royal Canada Mounted Police

12. What was one of the major developments of the late 19th century in Canada?

a. Joining the East and West by railroad

b. Construction of bridges

c. Granting voting rights

d. Constitution of the Police force

13. Who invested in the railroad project?

a. British investors

b. American investors

c. Both A & B

d. Neither A nor B

14. What was the colony at Quebec City renamed as?

a. The Quebec Province

b. The Province of Quebec City

c. The Province of Quebec

d. The Quebec City Province

15. What does CPR stand for?

a. Canada Pacific Railway

b. Canadian Pacific Rail-road

c. Canadian Pacific Rail

d. Canadian Pacific Railway   *Canadian unification*

16. How did French Catholics gain religious freedom?

a. The British government

b. The French population left over from Québec City

c. The Quebec Act   *1774*

d. The French Catholics

17. Who was the first French-Canadian Prime Minister?

a. Louis Riel

b. Sir Wilfrid Laurier   → *$5 BILL*

c. Robert Baldwin

d. Sir John Alexander Macdonald

18. When did Britain declare war on Germany?

    a. 1491

    b. 1419

    c. 1914

    d. 1941

19. Name the army formed by Ottawa of over 600,000 men.

    a. Canada Expeditionary Force

    b. Canadian Expeditionary Force

    c. The Canadian Corps

    d. Canadian Army

20. What is the name of the holiday celebrated for veterans who fought in World War I?

    a. Remembrance Day

    b. Canada Day

    c. Veteran's Day

    d. Dominion Day

21. Where were the first assembly elections held in Canada?

    a. Halifax, Nova Scotia   1 1758

    b. Prince Edward Island

    c. New Brunswick

    d. The Province of Quebec

22. Who was Dr. Emily Stowe?

a. The first woman to vote

b. The first woman to practice medicine in Canada, and begin the process to gain the vote for women.

c. The first woman to own property

d. The first female Member of Parliament Canada

23. Which province was the first to grant voting rights for women?

a. Manitoba   *1916*

b. Ottawa

c. Vancouver

d. Montreal

24. Who was the first female Member of Parliament to be elected in 1921?

a. Agnes MacPhal

b. Dr. Emily Stowe

c. Agnes MacPhail

d. Dr. Emily Stow

25. Which two other countries joined Canada in the British Commonwealth of Nations?

a. India and China

b. India and Austria

c. India and Australia

d. India and Germany

26. What was set up in 1934?

    a. The Stock Market of Canada

    b. Insurance Company

    c. The Bank of Canada

    d. A government instituted program

27. Who provided bombers and fighter planes in the Battle of Britain during World War II?

    a. Recognized Canadian Air Force

    b. Royal Canada Air Force

    c. Regional Canadian Air Force

    d. Royal Canadian Air Force

28. Which group made Lower Canada their home?

    a. English-speaking Protestant Loyalists

    b. The Black Loyalists

    c. The English speaking Catholics

    d. The French-speaking Catholics

29. Which country attacked Canadian occupied Vancouver and British Columbia during the World War II?

    a. Germany

    b. Russia

    c. Japan

    d. Italy

30. Where and when was oil discovered in Canada?

    a. In Alberta in 1947
    b. In Manitoba in 1947
    c. In Alberta in 1945
    d. In Manitoba in 1945

31. Name the most important trading policies initiated after the Second World War.

    a. General Agreement on Trading Tariffs
    b. General Agreement on Tariffs and Trade
    c. General Association of Trade and tariff
    d. General Agreement of Trade and Tariffs

32. What are the three levels of government in Canada?

    a. Local, Provincial/Territorial and Federal
    b. Federal, Municipal and Provincial/Territorial
    c. Local, National and County
    d. None of the above

33. Name the Canadian who invented the telephone?

    a. Graham Bell
    b. Healey Willan
    c. Donovan Bailey
    d. Wayne Gretzky

34. What type of government does Canada have?

a. Parliamentary Democracy

b. Democratic Parliament

c. House of Commons

d. Federalism

35. What is an important characteristic of cabinet ministers?

a. No confidence motions

b. The confidence of the cabinet

c. The confidence of the house

d. The confidence of the Prime Minister

36. What are the three branches of parliament?

a. The Sovereign, Congress and Senate

b. The Senate, Prime Minister and House of Commons

c. The House of Commons, Senate and Sovereign

d. President, Senate and House of Commons

37. Who serves the role of the Prime Minister in each province or territory?

a. Governor General

b. The Premier

c. The Commissioner

d. The Sovereign

38. Who is a representative of the federal government in the three Northern territories?

    a. The Prime Minister

    b. The Sovereign

    c. The Commissioner

    d. The Premier

39. Who serves as the Sovereign's representative in Canada?

    a. The Commissioner

    b. The Premier

    c. The Prime Minister

    d. Canada's Governor General

40. When are the Federal elections held every four years?

    a. The third Monday in October

    b. The third Monday in November

    c. The third Monday in August

    d. The first Monday in October

41. How many electoral districts are in Canada?

    a. 388

    b. 308

    c. 310

    d. 380

42. What is the minimum eligible age for a Canadian citizen to stand for election?

    a. 16

    b. 17

    c. 21

    d. 18

43. What civic right do you have as a Canadian citizen, above 18 years of age and registered on the voting list?

    a. Right to Federal matters

    b. Right to Earn an income

    c. Right to Judiciary

    d. Right to vote

44. What is the function of Elections Canada?

    a. Conducts elections and generates a database of politicians

    b. Conducts elections and gathers and stores voter information

    c. Conducts elections and gathers and stores election information

    d. Conducts elections and gathers and stores financial details of candidates fighting elections

45. Who becomes the Prime Minister after an election?

    a. The leader of the party with the most seats in the House of Commons

    b. The leader unanimously selected by his party members

    c. The Governor General decides the person to be Prime Minister

    d. The members of the parliament decides the person to be Prime Minister

46. How many major political parties are in Canada?

    a. Two

    b. Four

    c. Three

    d. Six

47. What are two levels of government besides the Federal government?

    a. Local and Federal Governments

    b. Provincial and Municipal Governments

    c. Local and Provincial governments

    d. Local and Municipal Governments

48. What is the highest court in Canada?

    a. Federal Court

    b. Supreme Court

    c. Provincial Court

    d. Court of Canada

49. Who is the Queen of Canada since 1952?

    a. Queen Elizabeth I

    b. Queen Victorian II

    c. Queen Elizabeth II

    d. Queen Victorian I

50. What are the two colors of the Canadian flag?

a. Red and White

b. White and Blue

c. Red and Blue

d. White and Black

51. Which is Canada's official Royal Flag?

a. The red and white pattern of the Canadian flag

b. The Military Flag of Canada

c. Union Jack of Britain

d. The Maple Leaf Flag

52. Which is Canada's most recognizable symbol?

a. The Union Jack

b. The Maple Leaf

c. The red and white pattern of the Canadian flag

d. The colors red and white

53. What is the English translation of Fleur-De-lys?

a. The Maple Leaf

b. The lily flower

c. The red and white colors

d. The Union Jack

54. Which province adopted the Fleur-De-Lys on their flag?

a. Quebec

b. Manitoba

c. British Columbia

d. New Brunswick

55. What does the official coat of arms represent?

a. The beauty of Canada

b. The honour and pride of Canada

c. The Government of Canada

d. The different immigrants of Canada

56. Where is the Canadian Parliament located?

a. Vancouver

b. Montreal

c. Toronto

d. Ottawa

57. Which is the most prominent building in Ottawa?

a. National Assembly

b. Center Block

c. The Peace Tower

d. The Parliament buildings

58. Name the most popular sport in Canada?

a. Hockey (Ice hockey)

b. Lacrosse

c. Soccer

d. Baseball

59. What was the symbol of the Hudson's Bay Company, and became the official emblem of St. Jean Baptiste Society in 1834?

a. The Red and White colors

b. The Maple Leaf

c. The Coat of Arms

d. The Beaver

60. Which is the highest military honour in Canada?

    a. The Victoria Cross

    b. The Coat of Arms

    c. Fleur-De-Lys

    d. The Maple Leaf medal

61. What year did the official Language Act pass?

    a. 1966

    b. 1699

    c. 1969

    d. 1996

62. Which important trade agreement did Canada sign in 1994?

    a. The North American Free Trade Agreement (NAFTA)

    b. General Agreement on Trade and Tariff (GATT)

    c. National Agency for Free Trade Agreement (NAFTA)

    d. National Agreement on Free Trade   (NAFT)

63. Which organization, made up of eight nations, is Canada a member of?

    a. North American group of nations

    b. International group of nations

    c. G8 group of nations

    d. G15 group of nations

64. What percentage of the workforce does Canada's service industry employ?

   a. 57

   b. 75

   c. 73

   d. 72

65. Canada is a world leader in which of the following?

   a. Largest number of industries

   b. Production of Automobiles

   c. Distribution of technology-related equipment

   d. Exporting natural resources

66. What symbolizes the close ties between Canada and the US?

   a. The Peace Tower

   b. The Peace Arch in Blaine, Washington,

   c. Confederation Bridge

   d. The world's longest undefended border

67. What is the land mass of Canada?

   a. 1000 million square kilometers

   b. 100 million square kilometers

   c. 10 million square kilometers

   d. 1 million square kilometers

68. How many unique and distinct regions are in Canada?

   a. Five

   b. Fifteen

   c. Fifty

   d. Fifty -one

69. What is the capital of Canada?

a. Montreal

b. Vancouver

c. Ottawa

d. Toronto

70. Where are the Great Lakes located?

a. The West Coast

b. Central Canada

c. The Prairie Provinces

d. The Northern Territories

71. Which is Canada's smallest Province?

a. Prince Edward Island

b. Nova Scotia, and

c. New Brunswick

d. Newfoundland and Labrador

72. Which province is situated in the Appalachian Mountain Range?

a. a. Prince Edward Island

b. b. Nova Scotia, and

c. c. New Brunswick

d. d. Newfoundland and Labrador

73. Which region is the manufacturing and industrial center of Canada?

a. The West Coast

b. Central Canada

c. The Prairie Provinces

d. The Northern Territories

74. Which province is known for its abundance of natural resources and fertile farmland?

    a. The West Coast

    b. Prince Edward Island

    c. The Prairie Provinces

    d. The Northern Territories

75. Which province is called the Land of the Midnight Sun?

    a. The West Coast

    b. Central Canada

    c. The Prairie Provinces,

    d. The Northern Territories

Answer Key

1. A
Two levels of government, formed in 1864 - 67 were the federal and provincial levels.

2. C
The Province of Canada was divided into Ontario and Quebec.

3. B
The British Parliament passed the British North America Act in 1867.

4. D
Canadians still celebrate what was once called Dominion Day, but now it is known simply as Canada Day.

5. A
Canada's first prime minister, Sir John A. Macdonald, was named in 1867. Scotland-born had come to Canada as a child.

6. C
John A. McDonald, Canada's first prime minister, is on the $10 bill.

7. A
After the Metis, led by Louis Riel, were defeated, Canada formed a new province, Manitoba.

8. C
Louis Riel was the leader of the uprising.

9. C
The North West Mounted Police (NWMP) was formed in 1873.

10. A
England won the decisive Battle of the Plains of Abraham at Québec city in 1759.

11. C
The Royal Canadian Mounted Police (RCMP) are Canada's national police force and one of the most recognizable symbols of Canadian authority.

12. A
A major development of the late 19th century was joining the East and West by railroad.

13. C
The Canadian Pacific Railway was financed by British and American investors, constructed by a European and Chinese labor force, and finished in 1885.

14. C
The British renamed the colony at Québec City "The Province of Quebec."

15. D
The CPR is a symbol of Canadian unification.

16. C
The Quebec Act in 1774 gave French Catholics religious freedom.

17. B
The first French-Canadian Prime Minister, Sir Wilfrid Laurier, whose portrait is on the $5 bill

18. C
When Britain declared war on Germany in 1914.

19. B
Ottawa formed the Canadian Expeditionary Force, comprised of over 600,000 men.

20. A
Canadians remember veterans each year on November 11th, which is called Remembrance Day.

21. A
1758 saw the first representative assembly elected in Halifax, Nova Scotia.

22. B
Dr. Emily Stowe was the first woman to practice medicine in
Canada, and begin the process to gain the vote for women.

23. A
Manitoba granted women the right to vote in 1916.

24. C
The first female Member of Parliament, Agnes Macphail, was
elected, in 1921.

25. C
India and Australia joined Canada in the British Commonwealth of Nations.

26. C
The Bank of Canada was set up in 1934, which brought stability to the failing economy.

27. D
The Royal Canadian Air Force (RCAF) provided bombers and
fighter planes in the Battle of Britain.

28. A
In Lower Canada, English-speaking Protestant Loyalists
made their homes.

29. C
In the Pacific, Japan attacked Canadian occupied Vancouver
and British Columbia.

30. A
Oil was discovered in Alberta in 1947.

31. B
The most important trade agreement was the General Agreement on Tariffs and Trade (GATT).

32. B
The three levels of government in Canada are Municipal,
Provincial/Territorial and Federal.

33. A
Alexander Graham Bell invented the telephone.

34. A
Canada's government is known as a Parliamentary Democracy.

35. C
The so-called "confidence of the House" is an important requirement of cabinet ministers.

36. C
These three branches are the Sovereign (King or Queen), the Senate, and the House of Commons.

37. B
An individual known as the Premier serves the role as the Prime Minister in each province or territory.

38. C
In the three territories, the Commissioner is a representative of the federal government.

39. D
Canada's Governor General serves as the Sovereign's representative, for a term, usually limited to five years.

40. A
Federal elections in Canada are held every four years on the third Monday in October.

41. B
There are 308 electoral districts in Canada,

42. D
The minimum age for a Canadian citizen to stand for election is 18.

43. D
Canadian Citizens have the right to vote if they are at least 18 years of age and registered on the voting list.

44. B
Elections Canada conducts elections, gathers and stores voter information.

45. A
After the voting is cast and the election is over, the leader of the party with the most seats in the House of Commons is appointed by the Governor General. The leader of this party becomes the Prime Minister.

46. C
There are three major parties in Canada: The Conservative Party, the New Democratic Party, and the Liberal Party.

47. B
Two levels of government, in addition to the Federal government are the Municipal and Provincial governments.

48. B
The highest court in Canada is the Supreme Court.

49. C
Queen Elizabeth II has been the Queen of Canada since 1952.

50. A
The Canadian flag is a red and white maple leaf pattern.

51. C
The Union Jack of Britain is Canada's official Royal Flag.

52. B
The Maple Leaf is Canada's most recognizable symbol.

53. B
French for "the lily flower," the Fleur-De-Lys

54. A
Quebec adopted the Fleur-De-Lys on its Provincial flag.

55. B
Canada's official coat of arms represents national honor and pride.

56. D
Canada's Parliament buildings are located in Ottawa, Ontario

57. D
The Parliament Buildings are the most prominent buildings in Ottawa.

58. A
Hockey is Canada's most popular sport.

59. D
The beaver, a former symbol of the Hudson's Bay Company, became the official emblem of St. Jean Baptiste Society in 1834.

60. A
The Victoria Cross is the highest military honor available in Canada.

61. C
The Official Language Act passed in 1969.

62. A
Canada signed the North American Free Trade Agreement (NAFTA) of 1994.

63. C
Canada is part of the G8 group of Nations. The Group of Eight refers to the group of eight highly industrialized nations—France, Germany, Italy, the United Kingdom, Japan, the United States, Canada, and Russia

64. B
Canada's service industry is responsible for employing more than 75% of Canada's workforce.

65. D
Canada is one of the world leaders in exporting natural resources.

66. B
The Peace Arch in Blaine, Washington, symbolizes the close ties between Canada and the U.S.

67. C
At roughly 10 million square kilometers, Canada is the second largest country on earth.

68. A
Canada is made up of five unique and distinct regions.

69. C
The Capital of Canada is Ottawa

70. B
The Great Lakes (Ontario, Erie, Huron, Michigan, Superior) are also located in Southern Ontario.

71. A
Prince Edward Island is Canada's smallest Province.

72. C
New Brunswick is situated in the Appalachian Mountain Range.

73. B
Central Canada is the manufacturing and industrial center of Canada.

74. C
The Prairie Provinces are known for their abundance of natural resources and rich, fertile farmland.

75. D
The Northern Territories is often called the "Land of the Midnight Sun" due to its periods of long summer and short winter days.

How to Prepare for a Test

MOST STUDENTS HIDE THEIR HEADS AND PROCRASTINATE WHEN FACED WITH PREPARING FOR AN EXAM, HOPING THAT SOMEHOW THEY WILL BE SPARED THE AGONY, ESPECIALLY IF IT IS A BIG ONE THAT THEIR FUTURES RELY ON. Avoiding a test is what many students do best and unfortunately, they suffer the consequences because of their lack of preparation.

Test preparation requires strategy and dedication. It is the perfect training ground for a professional life. Besides having several reliable strategies, successful students also has a clear goal and know how to accomplish it. These tried and true concepts have worked well and will make your test preparation easier.

The Study Approach

Take responsibility for your own test preparation.

It is a common - but big - mistake to link your studying to someone else's. Study partners are great, but only if they are reliable. It is your job to be prepared for the test, even if a study partner fails you. Do not allow others to distract you from your goals.

Prioritize the time available to study

When do you learn best, early in the day or at night? Does your mind absorb and retain information most efficiently in small blocks of time, or do you require long stretches to get the most done? It is important to figure out the best blocks of time available to you when you can be the most productive. Try to consolidate activities to allow for longer periods of study time.

Find a quiet place where you will not be disturbed

Do not try to squeeze in quality study time in any old location. Find a quiet place with a minimum of distractions, such as the library, a park or even the laundry room. Good lighting is essential and you need to have comfortable seating and a desk surface large enough to hold your materials. It is probably not a great idea to study in your bedroom. You might be distracted by clothes on the floor, a book you have been planning to read, the telephone or something else. Besides, in the middle of studying, that bed will start to look very comfortable. Whatever you do, avoid using the bed as a place to study since you might fall asleep to avoiding studying!

The exception is flashcards. By far the most productive study time is sitting down and studying and studying only. However, with flashcards you can carry them with you and make use of odd moments, like standing in line or waiting for the bus. This isn't as productive, but it really helps and is definitely worth doing.

Determine what you need to study

Gather together your books, your notes, your laptop and any other materials needed to focus on your study for this exam. Ensure you have everything you need so you don't waste time. Remember paper, pencils and erasers, sticky notes, bottled water and a snack. Keep your phone with you if you need it to find essential information, but keep it turned off so others can't distract you.

Have a positive attitude

It is essential that you approach your studies for the test with an attitude that says you will pass it. And pass it with flying colors! This is one of the most important keys to successful studying. Believing that you are capable helps you to become capable.

The Strategy of Studying

Review class notes

Stay on top of class notes and assignments by reviewing them frequently and regularly and regularly. Re-writing notes can be a terrific study trick, as it helps lock in information. Pay special attention to any comments that have been made by the teacher. If a study guide has been made available as part of the class materials, use it! It will be a valuable tool to use for studying.

Estimate how much time you will need

If you are concerned about the amount of time you have available it is a good idea to set up a schedule so that you do not get bogged down on one section and end without enough time left to study other things. Remember to schedule break time, and use that time for a little exercise or other stress reducing techniques.

Test yourself to determine your weaknesses

Look online for additional assessment and evaluation tools available like practice questions for a particular subject. Visit our website https://www.test-preparation.ca for test tips and more practice questions. Once you have determined your weaknesses, you can focus on these, and just brush up on the other areas of the exam.

Mental Prep – How to Psych Yourself Up for a Test

Since tests are often a big factor in your final grade or acceptance into a program, it is understandable taking tests is stressful for many students. Even students who know they have learned the required material find their minds going blank as they stare at the test booklet. You can avoid test anxiety by preparing yourself mentally. One easy way to overcome that anxiety is to prepare mentally for the test with a few simple techniques. **Do not procrastinate**

Study the material for the test when it becomes available, and continue to review the material until the test day. By waiting until the last minute and trying to cram for the test the night before, you actually increase anxiety. This leads to negative self-talk, which becomes self-fulfilling. Telling yourself "I can't learn this. I am going to fail" is a pretty sure indication that you are right.

Positive self-talk.

Positive self-talk drowns out negative self-talk and to increases your confidence level. Whenever you begin feeling overwhelmed or anxious about the test, remind yourself that you have studied enough, you know the material and that you will pass the test. Both negative and positive self-talk are really just your fantasy, so why not choose to be a winner?

Do not compare yourself to others.

Do not compare yourself to other students. Instead, focus on your strengths and weaknesses and prepare accordingly. Regardless of how others perform, your performance is the only one that effects your grade. Comparing yourself to others increases your anxiety and negative self-talk before the test.

Visualize.

Make a mental image of yourself taking the test. You know the answers and feel relaxed. Visualize doing well on the test and having no problems with the material. Visualizations can increase your confidence and decrease the anxiety you might otherwise feel before the test. Instead of thinking of this as a test, see it as an opportunity to demonstrate what you have learned!

Avoid negativity.

Worry is contagious and viral - once it gets started it builds on itself. Cut it off before it gets to be a problem. Even if you are relaxed and confident, being around anxious, worried classmates might cause you to start feeling anxious. Before the test, tune out the fears of classmates. Feeling anxious and worried before an exam is normal, and every student experiences those feelings at some point. But you cannot allow these feelings to interfere with your performance. Practicing mental preparation techniques and remembering that the test is not the only measure of your academic performance will ease your anxiety and ensure that you perform at your best.

How to Take a Test

EVERYONE KNOWS THAT TAKING AN EXAM IS STRESSFUL, BUT IT DOES NOT HAVE TO BE THAT BAD! There are a few simple things that you can do to increase your score on any type of test. Take a look at these tips and consider how you can incorporate them into your study time.

OK - so you are in the test room - Here is what to do!

Reading the Instructions

This is the most basic point, but one that, surprisingly, many students ignore and it costs big time! Since reading the instructions is one of the most common, and 100% preventable mistakes, we have a whole section just on reading instructions.

Pay close attention to the sample questions. Almost all standardized tests offer sample questions, paired with their correct solutions. Go through these to make sure that you understand what they mean and how they arrived at the correct answer. Do not be afraid to ask the test supervisor for help with a sample that confuses you, or instructions that you are unsure of.

Tips for Reading the Question

We could write pages and pages of tips just on reading the test questions. Here are a few that will help you the most.

- **Think first.** Before you look at the answer, read and think about the question. It is best to try to come up with the correct answer before you look at the options. This way, when the test-writer tries to trick you with a close answer, you will not fall for it.

• **Make it true or false.** If a question confuses you, then look at each answer option and think of it as a "true" "false" question. Select the one that seems most likely to be "true."

• **Mark the Question.** Don't be afraid to mark up the test booklet. Unless you are specifically told not to mark in the booklet, use it to your advantage.

• **Circle Key Words.** As you are reading the question, underline or circle key words. This helps you to focus on the most critical information needed to solve the problem. For example, if the question said, "Which of these is not a synonym for huge?" You might circle "not," "synonym" and "huge." That clears away the clutter and lets you focus on what is important.

• **Always underline these words:** all, none, always, never, most, best, true, false and except.

• **Eliminate.** Elimination is the best strategy for multiple choice answers *and* questions. If you are confused by lengthy questions, cross out anything that you think is irrelevant, obviously wrong, or information that you think is offered to distract you. Elimination is the most valuable strategy!

• **Do not try to read between the lines.** Usually, questions are written to be straightforward, with no deep, underlying meaning. Generally, the simple answer really is the correct answer. Do not over-analyze!

How to Take a Test - The Basics

Some sections of the test are designed to assess your ability to quickly grab the necessary information; this type of exam makes speed a priority. Others are more concerned with your depth of knowledge, and how accurate it is. When you start a new section of the test, look it over to determine whether the test is for speed or accuracy. If the test is for speed (a lot of questions and a short time), your strategy is clear; answer as many questions as quickly as possible.

The Citizenship test does NOT penalize for wrong answers, so if all else fails, guess and make sure you answer every question.

Make time your friend

Budget your time from the beginning until you are finished, and stick to it! The time for each section will be included in the instructions.

Easy does it

One smart way to tackle a test is to locate the easy questions and answer those first. This is a time-tested strategy that never fails, because it saves you a lot of unnecessary anxiety. First, read the question and decide if you can answer it in less than a minute. If so, complete the question and go to the next one. If not, skip it for now and continue to the next question. By the time you have completed the first pass through this section of the exam, you will have answered a good number of questions. Not only does it boost your confidence, relieve anxiety and kick your memory up a notch, you will know exactly how many questions remain and can allot the rest of your time accordingly. Think of doing the easy questions first as a warm-up!

Do not watch your watch

At best, taking an important exam is an uncomfortable situation. If you are like most people, you might be tempted to subconsciously distract yourself from the task at hand. One of the most common ways is by becoming obsessed with your watch or the wall clock. Do not watch your watch! Take it off and place it on the top corner of your desk, far enough away that you will not be tempted to look at it every two minutes. Better still, turn the watch face away from you. That way, every time you try to sneak a peek, you will be reminded to refocus your attention to the task at hand. Give yourself permission to check your watch or the wall clock after you complete each section. Focus on answering the questions, not on how many minutes have elapsed since you last looked at it.

Divide and conquer

What should you do when you come across a question that is so complicated you may not even be certain what is being asked? As we have suggested, the first time through, skip the question. At some point, you will need to return to it and get it under control. The best way to handle questions that leave you feeling so anxious you can hardly think is by breaking them into manageable pieces. Solving smaller bits is always easier. For complicated questions, divide them into bite-sized pieces and solve these smaller sets separately. Once you understand what the reduced sections are really saying, it will be much easier to put them together and get a handle on the bigger question. This may not work with every question - see below for how to deal with questions you can-not break down.

Reason your way through the toughest questions

If you find that a question is so dense you can't figure out how to break it into smaller pieces, there are a few strategies that might help. First, read the question again and look for hints. Can you re-word the question in one or more differ-ent ways? This may give you clues. Look for words that can function as either verbs or nouns, and try to figure out what the questions is asking from the sentence structure. Re-member that many nouns in English have several different meanings. While some of those meanings might be related, sometimes they are completely distinct. If reading the sen-tence one way does not make sense, consider a different definition or meaning for a key word.

The truth is, it is not always necessary to understand a question to arrive at a correct answer! The most successful strategy for multiple choice is Elimination. Frequently, at least one answer is clearly wrong and can be crossed off the list of possible correct answers. Next, look at the remaining answers and eliminate any that are only partially true. You may still have to flat-out guess from time to time, but using the process of elimination will help you make your way to the correct answer more often than not - even when you don't know what the question means!

Do not leave early

Use all the time allotted to you, even if you can't wait to get out of the testing room. Instead, once you have finished, spend the remaining time reviewing your answers. Go back to those questions that were most difficult for you and review your response. Another good way to use this time is to return to multiple-choice questions in which you filled in a bubble. Do a spot check, reviewing every fifth or sixth question to make sure your answer coincides with the bubble you filled in. This is a great way to catch yourself if you made a mistake, skipped a bubble and therefore put all your answers in the wrong bubbles!

Become a super sleuth and look for careless errors. Look for questions that have double negatives or other odd phrasing; they might be an attempt to throw you off. Careless errors on your part might be the result of skimming a question and missing a key word. Words such as "always," "never," "sometimes," "rarely" and the like can give a strong indication of the answer the question is really seeking. Don't throw away points by being careless!

Just as you budgeted time at the beginning of the test to allow for easy and more difficult questions, be sure to budget sufficient time to review your answers. On essay questions and math questions where you are required to show your work, check your writing to make sure it is legible.

Math questions can be especially tricky. The best way to

double check math questions is by figuring the answer using a different method, if possible.

Here is another terrific tip. It is likely that no matter how hard you try, you will have a handful of questions you just are not sure of. Keep them in mind as you read through the rest of the test. If you can't answer a question, looking back over the test to find a different question that addresses the same topic might give you clues.

We know that taking the test has been stressful and you can hardly wait to escape. Just Leaving before you double-check as much as possible can be a quick trip to disaster. Taking a few extra minutes can make the difference between getting a bad grade and a great one. Besides, there will be lots of time to relax and celebrate after the test is turned in.

In the Test Room – What you MUST do!

If you are like the rest of the world, there is almost nothing you would rather avoid than taking a test. Unfortunately, that is not an option if you want to pass. Rather than suffer, consider a few attitude adjustments that might turn the experience from a horrible one to…well, an interesting one! Take a look at these tips. Simply changing how you perceive the experience can change the experience itself.

You have to take the test - you can't change that. What you can change, and the only thing that you can change, is your attitude -so get a grip - you can do it!

Get in the mood

After weeks of studying, the big day has finally arrived. The worst thing you can do to yourself is arrive at the test site feeling frustrated, worried, and anxious. Keep a check on your emotional state. If your emotions are shaky before a test it can determine how well you do on the test. It is extremely important that you pump yourself up, believe in yourself, and use that confidence to get in the mood!

Don't fight reality

Students often resent tests, and with good reason. After all, many people do not test well, and they know the grade they end with does not accurately reflect their true knowledge. It is easy to feel resentful because tests classify students and create categories that just don't seem fair. Face it: Students who are great at rote memorization and not that good at actually analyzing material often score higher than those who might be more creative thinkers and balk at simply memorizing cold, hard facts. It may not be fair, but there it is anyway. Conformity is an asset on tests, and creativity is often a liability. There is no point in wasting time or energy being upset about this reality. Your first step is to accept the reality and get used to it. You will get higher marks when you realize tests do count and that you must give them your best effort. Think about your future and the career that is easier to achieve if you have consistently earned high grades. Avoid negative energy and focus on anything that lifts your enthusiasm and increases your motivation.

Get there early enough to relax

If you are wound up, tense, scared, anxious, or feeling rushed, it will cost you. Get to the exam room early and relax before you go in. This way, when the exam starts, you are comfortable and ready to apply yourself. Of course, you do not want to arrive so early that you are the only one there. That will not help you relax; it will only give you too much time to sit there, worry and get wound up all over again.

If you can, visit the room where you will be taking your exam a few days ahead of time. Having a visual image of the room can be surprisingly calming, because it takes away one of the big 'unknowns'. Not only that, but once you have visited, you know how to get there and will not be worried about getting lost. Furthermore, driving to the test site once lets you know how much time you need to allow for the trip. That means three potential stressors have been eliminated all at once.

Get it down on paper

One advantage of arriving early is that it allows you time to recreate notes. If you spend a lot of time worrying about whether you will be able to remember information like names, dates, places, and mathematical formulas, there is a solution for that. Unless the exam you are taking allows you to use your books and notes, (and very few do) you will have to rely on memory. Arriving early gives to time to tap into your memory and jot down key pieces of information you know that will be asked. Just make certain you are allowed to make notes once you are in the testing site; not all locations will permit it. Once you get your test, on a small piece of paper write down everything you are afraid you will forget. It will take a minute or two but by dumping your worries onto the page you have effectively eliminated a certain amount of anxiety and driven off the panic you feel.

Get comfortable in your chair

Here is a clever technique that releases physical stress and helps you get comfortable, even relaxed in your body. You will tense and hold each of your muscles for just a few seconds. The trick is, you must tense them hard for the technique to work. You might want to practice this technique a few times at home; you do not want an unfamiliar technique to add to your stress just before a test, after all! Once you are at the test site, this exercise can always be done in the rest room or another quiet location.

Start with the muscles in your face then work down your body. Tense, squeeze and hold the muscles for a moment or two. Notice the feel of every muscle as you go down your body. Scowl to tense your forehead, pull in your chin to tense your neck. Squeeze your shoulders down to tense your back. Pull in your stomach all the way back to your ribs, make your lower back tight then stretch your fingers. Tense your leg muscles and calves then stretch your feet and your toes. You should be as stiff as a board throughout your entire body.

Now relax your muscles in reverse starting with your toes. Notice how all the muscles feel as you relax them one by one. Once you have released a muscle or set of muscles, allow them to remain relaxed as you proceed up your body. Focus on how you are feeling as all the tension leaves. Start breathing deeply when you get to your chest muscles. By the time you have found your chair, you will be so relaxed it will feel like bliss!

Fight distraction

A lucky few are able to focus deeply when taking an important examination, but most people are easily distracted, probably because they would rather be any place else! There are several things you can do to protect yourself from distraction.

Stay away from windows.

If you sit near a window you are adding an unnecessary distraction.

Choose a seat away from the aisle so you do not become distracted by people who leave early. People who leave the exam room early are often the ones who fail. Do not compare your time to theirs.

Of course, you love your friends; that's why they are your friends! In the test room, however, they should become complete strangers inside your mind. Forget they are there. The first step is to physically distance yourself from friends or classmates. That way, you will not be tempted to glance at them to see how they are doing, and there will be no chance of eye contact that could either distract you or even lead to an accusation of cheating. Furthermore, if they are feeling stressed because they did not spend the focused time studying that you did, their anxiety is less likely to permeate your hard-earned calm.

Of course, you will want to choose a seat where there is sufficient light. Nothing is worse than trying to take an important examination under flickering lights or dim bulbs.

Ask the instructor or exam proctor to close the door if there is a lot of noise outside. If the instructor or proctor is unable to do so, block out the noise as best you can. Do not let anything disturb you.

The citizenship test does not allow any personal items in the exam room. Eat protein, complex carbohydrates and a little fat to keep you feeling full and to supercharge your energy. Nothing is worse than a sudden drop in blood sugar during an exam.

Do not allow yourself to become distracted by being too cold or hot. Regardless of the weather outside, carry a sweater, scarf or jacket if the air conditioning at the test site is set too high, or the heat set too low. By the same token, dress in layers so that you are prepared for a range of temperatures.

Watch Caffeine

Drinking a gallon of coffee or gulping a few energy drinks might seem like a great idea, but it is, in fact, a very bad one. Caffeine, pep pills or other artificial sources of energy are more likely to leave you feeling rushed and ragged. Your brain might be clicking along, all right, but chances are good it is not clicking along on the right track! Furthermore, drinking coffee or energy drinks will mean frequent trips to the rest room. This will cut into the time you should be spending answering questions and is a distraction in itself, since each time you need to leave the room you lose focus. Pep pills will only make it harder for you to think straight when solving complicated problems.

At the same time, if anxiety is your problem try to find ways around using tranquilizers during test-taking time. Even medically prescribed anti-anxiety medication can make you less alert and even decrease your motivation. Being motivated is what you need to get you through an exam. If your anxiety is so bad that it threatens to interfere with your ability to take an exam, speak to your doctor and ask for documentation. Many testing sites will allow non-distracting test rooms, extended testing time and other accommodations with a doctor's note that explains the situation is made available.

Keep Breathing

It might not make a lot of sense, but when people become anxious, tense, or scared, their breathing becomes shallow and, sometimes stop breathing all together! Pay attention to your emotions, and when you are feeling worried, focus on your breathing. Take a moment to remind yourself to breathe deeply and regularly. Drawing in steady, deep breaths energizes the body. When you continue to breathe deeply you will notice you exhale all the tension.

If you feel you need to, try rehearsing breathing at home. With continued practice of this relaxation technique, you will begin to know the muscles that tense up under pressure. Call these your "signal muscles." These are the ones that will speak to you first, begging you to relax. Take the time to listen to those muscles and do as they ask. With just a little breathing practice, you will get into the habit of checking yourself regularly and when you realize you are tense, relaxation will become second nature.

Avoid Anxiety Before a Test

Manage your time effectively

This is a key to your success! You need blocks of uninterrupted time to study all the pertinent material. Creating and maintaining a schedule will help keep you on track, and will remind family members and friends that you are not available. Under no circumstances should you change your blocks of study time to accommodate someone else, or cancel a study session to do something more fun. Do not interfere with your study time for any reason!

Relax

Use whatever works best for you to relieve stress. Some folks like a good, calming stretch with yoga, others find expressing themselves through journaling to be useful. Some hit the floor for a series of crunches or planks, and still others take a slow stroll around the garden. Integrate a little relaxation time into your schedule, and treat that time, too, as sacred.

Eat healthy

Instead of reaching for the chips and chocolate, fresh fruits and vegetables are not only yummy but offer nutritional benefits that help to relieve stress. Some foods accelerate stress instead of reducing it and should be avoided. Foods that add to higher anxiety include artificial sweeteners, candy and other sugary foods, carbonated sodas, chips, chocolate, eggs, fried foods, junk foods, processed foods, red meat, and other foods containing preservatives or heavy spices. Instead, eat a bowl of berries and some yogurt!

Get plenty of ZZZZZZZs

Do not cram or try to do an all-nighter. If you created a study schedule at the beginning, and if you have stuck with that schedule, have confidence! Staying up too late trying to cram in last-minute bits of information is going to leave you exhausted the next day. Besides, whatever new information you cram in will only displace all the important ideas you've spent weeks learning. Remember: You need to be alert and fully functional the day of the exam

Have confidence in yourself!

Everyone experiences some anxiety when taking a test, but exhibiting a positive attitude banishes anxiety and fills you with the knowledge you really do know what you need to know. This is your opportunity to show how well prepared you are. Go for it!

Do not chitchat with friends

Let your friends know ahead of time that it is not anything
personal, but you are going to ignore them in the test room!
You need to find a seat away from doors and windows, one
that has good lighting, and get comfortable. If other students are worried their anxiety could be detrimental to you;
of course, you do not have to tell your friends that. If you
are afraid they will be offended, tell them you are protecting
them from your anxiety!

Common Test-Taking Mistakes

Taking a test is not much fun at best. When you take a
test and make a stupid mistake that negatively affects your
grade, it is natural to be very upset, especially when it is
something that could have been easily avoided. So what are
some of the common mistakes that are made on tests?

Put your name on the test!

How could you possibly forget to put your name on a test?
You would be amazed at how often that happens. Very often,
tests without names are thrown out immediately, resulting
in a failing grade.

Marking the wrong multiple-choice answer

It is important to work at a steady pace, but that does not mean bolting through the questions. Be sure the answer you are marking is the one you mean to. If the bubble you need to fill in or the answer you need to circle is 'C', do not allow yourself to get distracted and select 'B' instead.

Answering a question twice

Some multiple-choice test questions have two very similar answers. If you are in too much of a hurry, you might select them both. Remember that only one answer is correct, so if you choose more than one, you have automatically failed that question.

Mishandling a difficult question

We recommend skipping difficult questions and returning to them later, but beware! First, be certain that you do return to the question. Circling the entire passage or placing a large question mark beside it will help you spot it when you are reviewing your test. Secondly, if you are not careful to skip the question, you can mess yourself up badly. Imagine that a question is too difficult and you decide to save it for later. You read the next question, which you know the answer to, and you fill in that answer. You continue to the end of the test then return to the difficult question only to discover you didn't actually skip it! Instead, you inserted the answer to the following question in the spot reserved for the harder one, thus throwing off the remainder of your test!

Incorrectly Transferring an answer from scratch paper

This can happen easily if you are trying to hurry! Double check any answer you have figured out on scratch paper, and make sure what you have written on the test itself is an exact match!

Thinking too much

Generally, your first thought is your best thought. If you worry yourself into insecurity, your self-doubts can trick you into choosing an incorrect answer when your first impulse was the right one!

Conclusion

CONGRATULATIONS! You have made it this far because you have applied yourself diligently to practicing for the exam and no doubt improved your potential score considerably! Passing your up-coming exam is a huge step in a journey that might be challenging at times but will be many times more rewarding and fulfilling. That is why being prepared is so important.

Good Luck!

FREE Ebook Version

Download a FREE Ebook version of the publication!

Suitable for tablets, iPad, iPhone, or any smart phone.

Go to
http://tinyurl.com/lfr25dj

Notes

1 http://www.cic.gc.ca/english/citizenship/become-eligibil-ity.asp

2. Oath of Citizenship. In Wikipedia. Retrieved November 12, 2014 from, http://en.wikipedia.org/wiki/Oath_of_Citizenship_(Canada)

3. Inuit. In Wikipedia. Retrieved November 12, 2014 from, http://en.wikipedia.org/wiki/Inuit

4. Canadian Statutory Holidays. In Wikipedia. Retrieved November 12, 2014 from, http://en.wikipedia.org/wiki/Public_holidays_in_Canada